"I have known Rex Hou the most disciplined, self met. He truly understands ... that are needed to take personal responsibility for your own life."

> - Jim Brewer, CEO, MasterThink, Ltd

"All leadership begins with self-leadership, and if you can't lead yourself, you shouldn't be leading others. Rex Houze has been leading and teaching others to lead for a generation. I first learned from him in the 1970s in a seminar in Chicago. He's a wise man; now's your chance to learn from him."

> - Jim Cathcart, author of the bestsellers:
> *The Acorn Principle* & *Relationship Selling.*

"We were excited to hear that Rex was publishing his third book and plan to use it with our entire marketing organization! His first two books were a big hit with our group, and people continually quote from them. We were fortunate enough to have Rex speak at several of our events ... which reinforced the teaching from his books! We highly recommend that all sales and/or marketing organizations ... as well as individuals ... utilize Rex's knowledge from all three of his published books and recommend that you invite him to speak to your group!"

> - Jody & Kathy Victor, MarkerNET, Inc.

"*Developing Personal Leadership* starts with the core ingredient of any successful person (winning attitude) and concludes with the critical overarching requirement for sustaining lasting and impactful leadership (integrity). Follow the concepts presented in this book from a life-long leader and create your own personal pattern of greater leadership."

> - Boyd Ober, President, Leadership Resources

"Rex Houze produces leadership development wisdom and common sense suggestions based on decades of experience. In my experience with Rex in conversations and in workshops he has conducted for HomeVestors over the last 5 years, he has always delivered experiences that transforms our team and creates the foundation that encourages us to achieve more than we would have without his leadership. I highly recommend this book to have Rex make a positive impact on the development of your team."

- Ken Channell, Co-President, HomeVestors of America, America's Number 1 HouseBuyer

"The foundational principles of leadership Houze presents in this text are absolutely crucial for success. The principles presented are true, easy to grasp, and relevant. He distills a lifetime of experience to give us lessons for leaders in all fields. We can better find the lessons of leadership through the precepts of a fellow who has helped thousands of people reach their full potential as leaders."

- Donna Stauber, Ph.D., CHES, Certified Life Coach, Rebuats, Inc.

"Rex has been associated with our company for many years and still continues to bring a fresh and exciting perspective to leadership and other business challenges we face. He has repeatedly earned the respect of our management team because he understands their business and provides relevant personal guidance and ongoing support. Rex is a most valuable resource and simply a great investment."

- Karl J. Warnke, Chairman, President & CEO, The Davey Tree Expert Company

"Rex shares some very practical approaches that are time-tested and easy to apply."

- Doug Dwyer, President & C.S.O. DreamMaker Bath & Kitchen

"If you want to learn how to walk on the moon, your best teacher would probably be one of the astronauts who actually walked there. If you want to learn how to lead, read this book by Rex Houze. He has magnificently walked the walk for the 30+ years I have known him... He has demonstrated his understanding in the real world and has studied the subject... probably more than any other man alive today. If Peter Drucker's teachings were explained as clearly as Rex's, Peter Drucker (1909-2005) would have been even more famous."

- Carl Bromer, Stellar Sales Training, Inc.

"Rex Houze's *Developing Personal Leadership* provides the eighteen essential ingredients for a complete personal leader. He describes in detail the real efforts required beyond the headlines commonly cited for effective leadership: positive mental attitude, goal-direction, self-motivation, and effective communication. The headlines are great, but the 'how-to' of Rex's eighteen steps provide the tools needed to develop what you desire---excellence of Personal Leadership."

- Paul J. Hindelang, Results Systems Corporation

"At a time when possessing effective leadership skills are critical to our personal and organizational success, this is a timely book that gives the reader the tools to accomplish these goals successfully. Through nearly twenty years of Rex's teaching, coaching, and mentoring my clients, I have achieved even greater results in goal setting, communication, finding our purpose, staying motivated, and the rewards of having a winning attitude. His work has encouraged me to be the best I can be and it will for you too!"

- Linda S. Carter, President, Resource Management Associates

"Talent and ability are not enough to achieve top performance. Understanding your talent and focusing it to achieve your highest personal goals requires the help of an equally capable coach. Rex Houze has done just that for thousands of people just like you. He has done it with powerful programs that harness his years of experience and practical counseling into exercises that engage your spirit and call forth the best of your talents into success in today's world."
     - Chuck Russell, Chairman & CEO, BestWork DATA

"I've known Rex for more than 20 years. His ability to turn complex information into valuable and simple user-friendly truth is exceptional. In his book, he boils valuable and life changing principles into clean and easy to apply disciplines that help anyone get to the 'next level' of greatness in any area of life. If you want to grow to a new level of achievement in your life and don't have time to read volumes of material on success, this is a must read."
     - Peter A. Dunn, President, Focus Consulting Group

"For the past 20 years, Rex Houze has epitomized a leadership coach. Rex's sound principles of leadership and communication has catapulted many careers. You will be stimulated, enlightened, and challenged from this writing."
     - Charles "C.I." Dixon, Dixon Motivational Management

Developing Personal Leadership

First Edition 2010

ISBN 978-0-9791108-4-9
Leadership/Business

Layout by AT Impact Consulting, LLC, Dallas, Texas
Published by PCG Business, a division of Pilot Communications Group, Inc. 317 Appaloosa Trail Waco, TX 76712

This book is dedicated to two future leaders who at the ages five and two are already demonstrating personal leadership characteristics. Although they cannot read yet, they love to be read to. They have great attitudes, are self-motivated and goal-directed, and even with a limited, but rapidly growing vocabulary, they are good at getting people to do what they want.

And, BOY, ARE THEY ENTHUSIASTIC!

Look out world – here come my granddaughters, Lily and Ava.

CONTENTS

Preface   13

How to Get the Most out of This Book   17

Part I - Positive Mental Attitude   19

  1. Developing a Winning Attitude   21
  2. Building Belief   33
  3. Increasing Self-Confidence   43
  4. Maintaining a High Energy Level   53
  5. Accepting Personal Responsibility   61

Part II - Self-Motivated   67

  6. Understanding Yourself and Those You Lead   69
  7. Achieving a High Level of Self-Motivation   79
  8. Keeping on with Perseverance   89

Part III - Goal-Directed   99

  9. Clarifying Goals   101
 10. Planning Your Future   119
 11. Stimulating Top Performance   127
 12. Maximizing Your Success   143
 13. Keeping the Main Thing the Main Thing   153

Part IV - Effective Communicator   175

 14. Bridging the Communication Gap   177
 15. Asking Questions and Listening   191
 16. Improving Performance with Feedback   201
 17. Using Authority and Influence Wisely   213
 18. Guarding Your Integrity   227

A Few More Thoughts   237

Making a Difference   239

About the Author   241

Index   243

Suggested Reading List   249

PREFACE

Think about the leaders who have had a positive impact on your life. Perhaps they had the "title" of Mom, Dad, Brother, Sister, Aunt, Uncle, or another relative. Perhaps they were a Teacher, Coach, Friend, Teammate, Co-worker or Boss. Perhaps they were an author.

Chances are it wasn't the President of the United States or the CEO of a large corporation or a politician or a movie star or any other "name in the news."

You don't need a fancy title or fame to be a leader. Personal leadership is about doing and being your best and having a positive influence on those you come in contact with.

The leaders in my life include my parents, especially my Mom; a little league baseball coach who died way too young; a Sunday school teacher who encouraged me to be a reader; a sixth grade teacher who played catch with me at recess; a high school teacher who encouraged me to apply my talents; my high school basketball coach who helped me be a better basketball player, not by teaching me specific skills, but by demanding my best performance at all times; two different mechanics who taught me many life lessons; an early boss who taught me to do the right thing because it was the right thing to do; and numerous friends and co-workers who have lifted me up in so many ways.

Few, if any, of these people would call themselves leaders – but they were to me and many others. I am a better person because of their influence, and that is what personal leadership is all about.

Since you are reading this Preface and will soon start reading *Developing Personal Leadership*, I know that regardless of whether or not you have a leadership title or of how good a leader you already are, you want to be better. Congratulations!

In this fast-paced world of 24/7 news, instant messaging, texting, Twittering, Facebooking, and so many other forms of social media, I strongly believe there's an even greater need for personal leadership than ever before. All of the people who have impacted my life have done so in a personal, not electronic way. Don't get me wrong. I believe in communicating and staying in touch via electronic means, but not exclusively. There must be a balance between personal and electronic communication.

My first introduction to formal leadership training was probably in the Cub Scouts, followed by the Boy Scouts. The first formal leadership development program I participated in was "Leadership in Action" – a program offered by the U.S. Jaycees. That was in 1968. As a result of that experience, I started reading all the self-help, leadership development books I could find including: *Think and Grow Rich*, *The Richest Man in Babylon*, *As a Man Thinketh*, *The Magic of Believing*, *The Magic of Thinking Big*, *Move Ahead with Possibility Thinking*, *Acres of Diamonds*, and many others.

In 1972, I purchased and applied the "Dynamics of Personal Leadership" program written by Paul J. Meyer, started my full-time leadership development business, and I have not looked back. I have spent decades learning and developing my personal leadership, and the rewards far outweigh the effort put forth.

I have seen and heard about thousands of people who have applied the principles I will share with you in this book and, as a result, have accomplished remarkable things in every area of their lives and the lives of those they touched.

When you have more of a positive mental attitude, are more self-motivated and goal-directed, and you are an effective communicator, people will be drawn to you, and you will have an impact on them in countless ways that you might never know.

I wrote this book as a way to "pay it forward" for all those who have helped me, and continue to help me develop personal leadership. My wish is that you will find one or more ideas in this book that you can and will apply in order to become an even better personal leader. You will make a difference whether you realize it or not.

Enthusiastically,
Rex Houze

HOW TO GET THE MOST OUT OF THIS BOOK

Success isn't bestowed; it is earned. When we refer to success or a successful life, we define success as the pursuit of a worthy goal or ideal. This definition means that the success is in the pursuit and is a journey, not a destination. As a result, when you set a goal and start pursuing it, or when you pursue a worthy ideal, the moment you start – you are successful.

By reading this book, you are pursuing your goal of developing personal leadership. As you begin your learning journey, I encourage you to make a commitment to not only read this book, but to study and apply the knowledge that is outlined in this book. To get the most out of this book, commit to the following 6 R's:

Read this book several times. The information contained within it will change your life.

Review the summaries at the end of each chapter often. They will serve as reminders of what is most important.

Repeat the affirmations at the end of each chapter. Make them a part of your daily life.

Remind yourself daily of what you are working toward -developing personal leadership.

Reap the rewards of your efforts by recognizing and appreciating the positive changes you see in both yourself and those around you.

Realize how far you have come on your journey toward developing personal leadership.

Part I

Positive Mental Attitude

....

Outlook. Perspective. Thoughts. Mindset. Frame of mind. Demeanor. Call it what you will, a positive mental attitude is a necessary component of personal leadership.

Our thoughts affect our outlook, our behavior, and ultimately our environment. They affect who we are and how we behave. Our thoughts help us excel or hold us back. They attract people to us or repel them. Our thoughts affect our attitude, and our attitude impacts our ability to develop our personal leadership.

Throughout the following five chapters, you will learn the key components of cultivating your own positive mental attitude. You will begin to see how a positive mental attitude will affect your self-image and how you have the power to choose your reaction to most situations. You will learn how to build belief in yourself and your abilities and will explore the benefits of having a high energy level and its impact on your overall success.

Your attitude is yours. You control it. Understanding this is vital to building a positive mental attitude. I challenge you to open your mind as you delve into the first part of this book and work toward developing personal leadership.

1.
Developing a Winning Attitude

"The greatest discovery of my generation is that a human being can alter his life by altering his attitudes of mind."

- William James

"A son and his father were walking on the mountains. Suddenly, his son falls, hurts himself, and screams, "AAAhhhh-hhhhhhh!!!" To his surprise, he hears the voice repeating, somewhere on the mountain, "AAAhhhhhhhhhhh!!!"

Curious, he yells, "Who are you?" He receives the answer, "Who are you?" And then he screams to the mountain, "I admire you!" The voice answers, "I admire you!" Angered at the response, he screams, "Coward!" He receives the answer, "Coward!"

He looks to his father and asks, "What's going on?" The father smiles and says, "My son, pay attention."

Again the man screams, "You are a champion!" The voice answers, "You are a champion!" The boy is surprised but does not understand.

Then the father explains, "People call this ECHO, but really this is LIFE. It gives you back everything you say or do. Our life is simply a reflection of our actions.

If you want more love in the world, create more love in your heart. If you want more competence in your team, improve your competence. This relationship applies to everything, in all aspects of life; life will give you back everything you have given to it."

ATTITUDE DEFINED

Our attitude controls our behaviors, and our behaviors ultimately affect our overall success. If you want to become a leader, you need to start acting like one.

An attitude is an outward expression of your inner thoughts and feelings. Change your attitude – change your life. Your attitude affects everything you do, which is good because your attitude is one of the few things you have complete control over.

What happens to you isn't nearly as important as your reaction to what happens to you. Likewise, your circumstances aren't nearly as important as your reaction to your circumstances. Your attitude today determines your success tomorrow and is the primary force that determines whether you succeed or fail.

For the sake of this discussion, attitude is defined as "a habit of thought." Thinking is defined as talking to yourself. When you are thinking, you are asking yourself questions and answering them in your head. In other words, the habitual way you talk to yourself forms your attitudes, and your attitudes affect everything you do.

By changing your thinking, you can change your attitude. By changing your attitude, you can change your behaviors and actions. When you change your behaviors and actions, you can change your results.

When your attitude improves, so do your circumstances. People have a tendency to adopt the attitudes of the people they spend time with. Attitudes are contagious, and there is only one thing more contagious than a good attitude - a bad attitude.

The most valuable asset you have is a positive mental attitude. W. Clement Stone, in his book *Success Through a Positive Mental Attitude*, wrote, "There is little difference in people, but that little difference makes a big difference. The little difference is attitude. The big difference is whether it is positive or negative."

HOW ATTITUDES ARE FORMED

People are creatures of habit. They tend to act in the same manner in similar circumstances. This can be good because it makes it easier to predict behavior. It can also be bad because people tend to change in three ways: slowly, rarely, and never. It's been said that if "you do what you've always done, you'll get what you always got." If you want to become better, you have to do something different.

People are creatures of habit mainly because of conditioning. We are conditioned by parents, teachers, and other authority figures and by what we see, what we hear, our past mistakes and failures, and other life experiences.

Perhaps you heard some of these phrases while growing up:

"Children should be seen and not heard."

"Don't bite off more than you can chew."

"Don't go where you're not wanted."

"Speak only when spoken to."

"Don't talk to strangers."

When you hear phrases such as these over and over again, they subconsciously become part of your self-image and help mold how you think and act.   These thoughts affect your attitude and, ultimately, your actions.   When these thoughts are negative, they will limit your success.

How successful can you be if you are thinking (at least on a subconscious level), "I should be seen and not heard. I shouldn't bite off more than I can chew. I shouldn't go where I'm not wanted. I should only speak when spoken to. I shouldn't talk with strangers."

Past mistakes and failures or embarrassing moments can hold you back. The fear of making a mistake or embarrassing yourself can be debilitating. It can limit your creativity, willingness to take risks, and ability to perform well.

In school, perhaps teachers in your early grades told you to "sit down, be quiet, and don't talk in class." Then in high school, a speech teacher requested you to "talk in class" impromptu, or without any preparation. How did you react? Did you experience sweaty palms, knees knocking, a knot in your stomach, and a dry throat? A lot of people never recover from these early negative experiences and, as a result, allow their fears to prevent their success.

Attitudes are vulnerable to stress, fatigue, and negative influences such as family, friends, co-workers, certain TV shows, and what you read. Guard your attitude carefully.

It has been proven that second-hand cigarette smoke can be damaging to your health. Likewise, second-hand words can be harmful to your attitude. Avoid conversations that are negative or otherwise toxic.

Instead, feed your attitudes through reading positive quotation books and other affirming books, by listening to inspirational/motivational CDs, and associating with positive, supportive people. Just as you drink water to flush the negative toxins out of your system, you need to do the same thing to the negative toxins that enter your mind.

ELIMINATE "IF ONLY" AND "WHAT IF" THINKING

You have probably heard people say, "If only I were taller, faster, had more money, completed college, spent more time with my children, lived somewhere else, etc." "If only" focuses on the past. It creates a "victim" mentality. You cannot do anything about the past, except learn from it. Spending time worrying about "if only" will keep you from doing something more productive.

"What if", in this context, is worrying unnecessarily about the future. "What if I lose my job? What if I have a financial set-back? What if I experience health problems? What if my spouse leaves me?"

When you become overly concerned about what might happen in the future, you waste valuable time that could be better utilized focusing on the present to enhance your future. It is okay to look at contingencies or ask, "What's the worst that could possibly happen?" Since you really cannot control the future, worrying about what might happen can mess with your attitude and keep you from being as productive as you would like to be. There is a difference between focusing on possible solutions and just focusing on the problems. Make sure you do the former.

In the words of Robert K. Cooper:
"To lead by example...
Love as if you'll live forever,
Work as if you have no need for money,
Dream as if no one can say no,
Have fun as if you never have to grow up,
Sing as if no one else is listening,
Care as if everything depends on your caring,
And raise a banner where a banner never flew."

ACTING YOUR WAY TO A BETTER ATTITUDE

It was mid-morning on a dreary day in Tallmadge, Ohio. It was early in my career, and I was struggling to get my business going. I hadn't made one phone call that morning, even though my goal was to make twenty by 9:00 a.m.

The phone rang and fellow franchisee Howard Tangler greeted me with, "What are you doing?" I told him, "Howard, I'm not going to lie to you; I'm sitting here shuffling prospect cards, feeling sorry for myself." He asked me if I had at least five prospect cards, and I told him I had several hundred. He told me to call any five and call him back in ten minutes. I called him back in less than ten minutes, and he asked me how it went. I said, "Fantastic!" He said, "Tell me about it." I had called five random prospects, talked with three of them, and scheduled an appointment with one of them. And, as a result, I went from feeling sorry for myself to feeling on top of the world.

Although your emotions are many times more powerful than your thoughts, they are more difficult to access because they are buried deeper in your psyche. Think of concentric circles. Your thoughts are located on the surface of the circle. The next circle contains your beliefs, the next your attitude, and the innermost circle contains your feelings or emotions. Your feelings or emotions will only cause you to take action when something is serious enough to reach that deep.

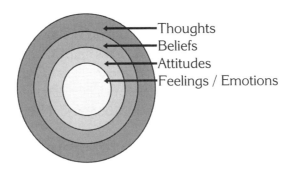

When you catch yourself procrastinating, or otherwise not acting, consciously think about some short-term action you can take immediately, within the hour, by the end of the day, etc. to eliminate procrastination and encourage action. When you are feeling sorry for yourself, take some short-term action. If you get disheartened or discouraged, take action. When you have a set-back, take some action. Taking action will give your attitude a boost, and once your attitude is boosted, it will have a tendency to take over.

Even if you don't have a choice about the circumstances you find yourself in, you do have a choice about your attitude toward the situation. The attitude you choose can change the outcome.

It is important to recognize that we will be no better tomorrow than we are today except for the books we read, the positive messages we listen to, and the people we associate with. What books are you reading? What personal or professional development CDs are you listening to? What seminars or workshops are you attending? In what ways are you getting better every day?

To improve your attitude and ultimately your results:

1. Look at all the things you do on a regular basis and pick one you'd like to improve.

2. Determine an action you can take to improve and take that action.

3. Repeat this process every day with the same area as long as needed or with a new area.

4. Say, "thank you" when people start noticing your improvement (be patient).

By devoting 10 minutes every day to continuous improvement, you will enjoy over 60 hours of improvement in a year. If you choose to only improve on weekdays, you will still enjoy over 40 hours of personal improvement. I'm confident you won't miss what you displace in those minutes.

YOUR GREATEST POWER

Your greatest power is your power to choose. You can choose your attitude, your thoughts, your reaction to situations, how you look, how you act, what you say, and how you say it. For the most part, you can choose your friends, who you associate with, how you spend your free time, how much energy you exert, your role models, the questions you ask, the books you read, the food you eat, your concerns and worries, and your relationships. Your daily – even moment to moment – choices will determine the kind of day you have and the kind of week, month, year, career, and life you will have. You can choose to:

1. Be positive or negative.

2. Be happy or sad.

3. Be caring or mean.

4. Be enthusiastic or dull.

5. Be ambitious or lazy.

6. Be goal-directed or adrift.

7. Be green and growing or ripe and rotting.

8. Focus on what you can do or what you can't do.

9. Help or hurt.

10. Build up or tear down.

11. Keep the main thing the main thing or do the wrong things.

12. Act your way to a new set of feelings or be frozen with procrastination or fear.

13. Take responsibility for your actions or make excuses.

14. Look for ways to learn and improve or be satisfied with the status quo.

15. Have fun or be glum.

16. Unleash someone's potential or squash it.

17. Do your best or settle for good enough.

18. Encourage or discourage.

19. Help people be right or point out how and why they are wrong.

20. Expect, encourage, & embrace change or resist change.

It is up to you to choose thoughts and actions that will help you improve your performance and results and enjoy the kind of success you want.

J. Martin Kohe, author of *Your Greatest Power* says:

"The greatest power a person possesses is the power to choose."

"Let us choose to believe something good can happen."

"You possess a potent force that you either use, or misuse, hundreds of times every day."

"Yes, we are all different: different customs, different foods, different mannerisms, different languages, but not so different that we cannot get along with one another, if we disagree without being disagreeable."

THE ROLE OF SELF-IMAGE IN SUCCESS

Dr. Maxwell Maltz, a plastic surgeon, developed a concept called "self-image psychology" in his best selling book, *Psycho-Cybernetics*. He discovered that many patients who had cosmetic or corrective plastic surgery continued to see themselves as ugly or disfigured. When scientists studied this phenomenon, they concluded that people have a subconscious and conscious mind.

Psycho-Cybernetics Model

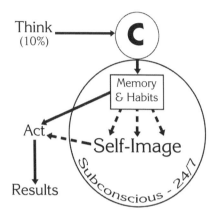

Your subconscious mind works 24/7. It is made up of your memory bank and self-image. It records everything you have ever heard, read, or said. Unlike the conscious mind, your subconscious mind cannot tell the difference between fact and fantasy. It believes everything it hears and stores it in your memory bank and/or self-image.

The conscious mind is where you do your thinking. It is working while you are awake. Most people only use their conscious mind about ten percent of their waking hours. This is true because your subconscious mind turns something into a habit, meaning it happens automatically and instinctively without having to think about it. Although this saves time, it causes a problem when you try to change a habit.

Your conscious mind explores your subconscious database to find the data that supports your thoughts or desired actions. If it is something you have done numerous times and turned into a habit, it will be in your memory bank, and you will perform the action the same way you have on numerous occasions.

However, if it is a new thought or desired action, the self-image portion of your subconscious mind comes into play. You will act based on what is in your self-image and get results accordingly. Your success, especially in new adventures, will be greatly determined by your self-image. It is a servo-mechanism that does whatever you tell it to do to the best of its ability.

Your self-image is developed by your thoughts: the books you read, what you listen to, your past experiences, and the input you receive from friends, business associates, and family members. Each positive experience puts a growth bump on your self-image. Each negative experience nicks or takes a chunk out of your self-image. As a result, it is important to focus on your strengths, have written and specific goals, and be mindful of your past accomplishments and victories. It is also important to feed your subconscious mind with positive input from the books you read, recordings you listen to, and the people you associate with. Your future success depends on it.

DEVELOPING A WINNING ATTITUDE - SUMMARY

✓ Your attitude today determines your success tomorrow and is the primary force that determines whether you succeed or fail.

✓ Your attitude drives your behavior, and your behavior determines your results.

✓ Overcoming past conditioning is one of the greatest challenges to developing a winning attitude.

✓ Your self-image acts as an accelerator or a governor.

✓ You are the beneficiary or victim of your choices.

DEVELOPING A WINNING ATTITUDE - AFFIRMATIONS

- ✓ I have a winning attitude.

- ✓ I can/have overcome my past conditioning.

- ✓ I will feed my attitude by associating with positive, supportive people.

- ✓ I continue to build a positive self-image with the books I read and the people I associate with.

- ✓ I make good choices that are helping me build a successful life.

2.
Building Belief

*"Whatever the mind of man can conceive
and believe, it can achieve."*

- W. Clement Stone

*In the early 1950's everyone thought it was impossible for
anyone to run a mile in under four minutes. The expectation
was that a sub-four minute mile was just NOT POSSIBLE;
it couldn't be done. Consequently, NO ONE ran a sub-four
minute mile.*

That is, until Roger Bannister.

*On May 6, 1954, at a meet in Oxford, England, Bannister
ran the mile in 3:59.4. He set his goal and achieved it.*

*The next month, that record was broken again by an Aus-
tralian runner and, in the following year, 20 other runners
turned in a sub-four minute mile. 20! With one exception,
nothing had changed. Not the shoes, the track, the weather,
the timing equipment, or the clothing. The only thing that
changed was the belief that it was possible to run a mile in
less than four minutes.*

BELIEVE TO SUCCEED

To achieve a goal, you need to first believe in your
ability to achieve it. Beliefs effect action. For example, once
Roger Bannister believed he could run a mile in under four
minutes, he succeeded.

A person's belief can be directed toward a product or
service, an industry, a profession, other people, and/or, most

importantly, toward themselves. People are not born with belief; it is learned and becomes a habitual way of thinking.

THE ROLE OF SELF-IMAGE AND SELF-ESTEEM IN SUCCESS

Your self-image and self-esteem determine what you are willing to try. Self-image is how you see yourself. It is formed from early childhood and continues to develop throughout your life. Positive experiences and feedback build your self-image, and negative experiences and feedback can, if you let it, damage or even destroy your self-image. Most children get a lot of positive feedback when they learn to walk, talk, eat with a spoon, etc. When we go to school, our self-image can be shaped by the kind of grades we get, relationships with our friends, and participation in extra-curricular activities. As we get older, life experiences shape our self-image, e.g. our work history, dating experiences, financial matters, and health issues.

Self-esteem, on the other hand, is the value you place on yourself and is mainly determined by your self-image. Since each of us is unique, we need to strive to be the best "me" we can be.

Positive reinforcement plays a significant role in who we are and who we become.

Tapping your potential starts with believing in yourself and what you are capable of accomplishing.

Believe that you deserve the best. Believe that you deserve to be happy, healthy, and successful. Believe that you have talents that will contribute to your family, your employer, your community, and society as a whole. Believe in your family. Believe in your co-workers. Believe in the organization you represent. Your subconscious mind will support your beliefs whether they are positive or negative, so it is important to make them positive.

Let me ask you, would you give up an arm, leg, or eye for a million dollars? I doubt it. Since we have two arms, two legs, two eyes, our sense of hearing, and many more body parts that we wouldn't sell for a million dollars, it stands to reason that we are worth millions, and we need to value ourselves accordingly.

HOW TO DEVELOP YOUR BELIEF

According to the theory of aerodynamics, and this may be readily demonstrated through experiments, the bumble bee is unable to fly. This is because the size, weight, and shape of his body, in relation to his wingspread, make flying impossible.

BUT the bumble bee, being ignorant of these scientific truths, goes ahead and flies anyway – and makes a little honey every day.

To develop belief, focus on your strengths instead of your weaknesses. Look at what you've accomplished in the past, your unique talents, what you've learned, and what you are capable of learning. Set small goals and achieve them. Use positive self-talk. Associate with positive people who believe in you and support you. Keep a journal.

DEVELOP YOUR ABILITIES

To develop your abilities, tap into your unlimited potential. It is widely believed that people only use a small percentage of their talents and abilities. Identify your talents and abilities and determine ways you can use them more often and, at the same time, strengthen them. A small increase in the use of your talents and abilities can pay big dividends.

To develop your abilities, start from where you are and get better. To do this, I suggest you follow the four Stages of Learning.

Stages of Learning

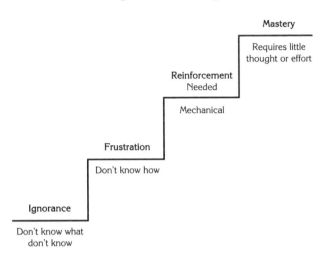

The first stage is ignorance. We don't know how to do something. Many times we don't even know that we don't know.

Once we determine that we want to learn how to do something, the second stage is frustration. We know that the task or skill is possible, but we don't know how to do it. This requires training. You can learn on your own or seek a mentor or other professional to teach you.

Stage three is the need for reinforcement. We know how to do it, but we need extra support, training, and/or reinforcement.

Stage four is mastery. We are able to do the task or perform the skill with little thought or effort.

Depending on the difficulty level of the task or skill

and our ability, we will usually reach stage three in a relatively short time period. Reaching mastery, however, takes a lot longer. That doesn't mean mastery isn't worth striving for because, in most cases, it is.

People who master a skill make it look easy. Tiger Woods mastered golf. LeBron James mastered basketball. Michael Phelps mastered swimming. Oprah Winfrey and Barbara Walters mastered interviewing. Mastery, however, does not mean you stop learning. As good as all these people are, they are still striving to improve. If people who are at the top of their "game" strive to improve, we need to do the same.

Regardless of the task you choose, you can improve your ability by reading a book, watching an instructional video or DVD, taking lessons, getting a mentor or coach, and by practicing purposely to get better. Determine where you stand now, set a goal to improve, practice purposely, and get feedback on your performance.

Remember, it is up to you to create your own success. Since you have a choice, why choose to be:

Average when you can be AWESOME?

Ordinary when you can be EXTRAORDINARY?

Mediocre when you can be MAGNIFICENT?

Poor when you can be PHENOMENAL?

Fair when you can be FANTASTIC?

Insignificant when you can be INCREDIBLE?

Ordinary when you can be OUTSTANDING?

Regular when you can be REMARKABLE?

Uncertain when you can be UNBELIEVABLE?

FEED YOUR MIND WITH THOUGHTS THAT SUPPORT YOUR BELIEF SYSTEM

Motivational speaker Zig Ziglar uses a term he calls SNIOP – Susceptible to the Negative Influence of Other People. All of us are susceptible to the influence of other people, particularly those who are important to us and those we see on a regular basis. Therefore, it is important to spend time with people who believe in us, support us, encourage us, and are a positive influence. By the same token, we need to avoid individuals that tend to put us down, fill our minds with negatives, and diminish our belief in ourselves and our abilities.

We also need to monitor our self-talk. The way we talk to ourselves effects our belief which, in turn, determines the results we get.

Eden Ryals, in a motivational film titled, "You Can Surpass Yourself," urged us not to "kid thyself." She maintains that the biggest enemies to the accomplishment of any goal are the lies we tell ourselves about our ability to accomplish it. Feed your mind by reviewing your strengths. Look at what you've accomplished in the past and determine how these accomplishments can help you achieve new goals.

Set a goal to master the skills you need to have a successful life. Get a mentor or coach to help you. Surround yourself with people who support you. Support your belief in yourself and your goals with positive self-talk.

THE ROLE OF VISUALIZATION IN A SUCCESSFUL LIFE

People think in word pictures. When we hear a word, we convert the word to a picture in our mind to give it meaning. This is done in nanoseconds. Since we already know how to convert words into pictures, it will be relatively easy to convert our goals into pictures. When you clearly picture in your mind the successful completion of a goal, it's just a matter a time before it will actually be accomplished.

For example, golfers visualize the path of the ball. Basketball players "see" the ball go through the hoop before it actually does. Architects "see" what a building will look like before it is built. Landscapers can picture what a property will look like before the first flower or tree is ever planted. Olympic trainers use visualization to assist athletes in mentally picturing a perfect performance before they physically compete.

Visualization will create the self-motivation needed to help you build your belief.

To aid in the visualization process, it is helpful to keep your goals visible. Place pictures that symbolize your accomplished goals in prominent places such as on your desk, your bathroom mirror, your refrigerator, the dash or visor of your car, and/or any other place where you will see them regularly. You can also create a "visualization board" out of poster board or cork board and place it where you can see it regularly. In regards to goals, "What you see is what you get."

DEVELOP, CULTIVATE, OR CREATE AN ABUNDANCE MENTALITY

In any endeavor, success is dependent on many factors. One factor that is often overlooked is the importance of having an abundance mentality. An "abundance mentality" is more than having a positive mental attitude. As we discussed in Chapter One, when you have a positive mental attitude, you look at how things can be done rather than why they can't be done. You believe that "where there's a will, there's a way." You look at possibilities and opportunities rather than obstacles and problems. This mindset is important for success in any endeavor.

An abundance mentality will take you beyond a positive mental attitude. It will eliminate small thinking and offset negative energy. Having an abundance mentality can mean the difference between success and failure, excellence and mediocrity, and prosperity and despair. People with an abundance mentality believe the following:

"The more I sell, the more there is to sell."

"The more I give, the more there is to give."

"The more I know, the more there is to know."

"People are great. They will help me reach my goals."

"If I need money, I'll find the money."

"If I need people, I'll find the people."

"If I need ideas, the ideas will come."

Individuals with an abundance mentality believe there are enough resources available to accomplish their goals. They also believe that their success doesn't mean failure for others. On the contrary, the more successful they are, the more others are affected in a positive way. They can be happy when friends and associates prosper. They can enter every business transaction with a "win/win" attitude since they win when their clients win.

To build your belief by boosting and enhancing your abundance mentality:

Make a commitment to continuous growth.
Set up a reading, listening, watching, and learning schedule. Participate in seminars and personal development programs.

Help others grow.
A wise philosopher once said, "When you help another per-

son get to the top of a mountain, you will arrive there also."
Teach people what you know. If you have a talent for coaching or teaching children, volunteer. Seeing people grow as a result of your efforts will enhance your abundance mentality and create a win/win situation.

Have a written, specific goals program.
Review your goals daily and update your action steps and accomplishments.

Utilize the synergy of a support group.
Join one or more organizations that have members who share your interest in personal and professional development and who will support you in the process.

To develop an abundance mentality, ask yourself:

- What are my dominating thoughts?

- What do I vividly imagine? Do I focus on abundance or scarcity? Success or failure? Results or activity?

- What do I want to happen? Health? Happiness? Prosperity? Peace of mind? Positive relationships?

We have 100 percent control over our thoughts and our behavior. When a negative thought creeps or rushes in, replace it with a positive thought. We can't always choose the situations we're in or the cards we're dealt, but we can choose our reaction to the situation or choose how to play the cards. When we control our thoughts, we control our outcomes.

Abundance starts in your mind. The more you think abundantly, the more abundance you can enjoy. The more abundance you enjoy, the more success you will enjoy.

"Watch your thoughts, for they become words.
Choose your words, for they become actions.
Understand your actions, for they become habits.

Study your habits, for they become your character.
Develop your character, for it becomes your destiny."

– Author Unknown

BUILDING BELIEF - SUMMARY

✓ Beliefs effect action.

✓ Tapping your potential starts with believing in yourself and what you are capable of accomplishing.

✓ The way we talk to ourselves effects our belief which, in turn, determines the results we get.

✓ Belief in yourself and a strong self-image and self-esteem go hand-in-hand.

✓ Taking positive action and getting positive results will build your belief in yourself.

BUILDING BELIEF- AFFIRMATIONS

✓ I believe in myself and my potential.

✓ I take positive action on my goals and what is important to me.

✓ I feed my mind positive thoughts on a daily basis.

✓ I use visualization to help build a successful life.

✓ I am cultivating an abundance mentality.

3.
Increasing Self-Confidence

"All other things being equal, self-confidence is often the single ingredient that distinguishes a successful person from someone less successful."

The business executive was deep in debt and could see no way out.

Creditors were closing in on him. Suppliers were demanding payment. He sat on the park bench, head in hands, wondering if anything could save his company from bankruptcy.

Suddenly an old man appeared before him. "I can see that something is troubling you," he said.

After listening to the executive's woes, the old man said, "I believe I can help you."

He asked the man his name, wrote out a check, and pushed it into his hand, saying, "Take this money. Meet me here exactly one year from today, and you can pay me back at that time."

Then, he turned and disappeared as quickly as he had come.

The business executive saw in his hand a check for $500,000, signed by John D. Rockefeller, then one of the richest men in the world!

"I can erase my money worries in an instant!" he realized. But instead, the executive decided to put the uncashed check in his safe. Just knowing it was there might give him the

strength to work out a way to save his business, he thought.

With renewed optimism, he negotiated better deals and extended terms of payment. He closed several big sales. Within a few months, he was out of debt and making money once again.

Exactly one year later, he returned to the park with the uncashed check. At the agreed upon time, the old man appeared. But just as the executive was about to hand back the check and share his success story, a nurse came running up and grabbed the old man.

"I'm so glad I caught him!" she cried. "I hope he hasn't been bothering you. He's always escaping from the rest home and telling people he's John D. Rockefeller."

And she led the old man away by the arm.

The astonished executive just stood there, stunned. All year long, he'd been wheeling and dealing, buying and selling, convinced he had half a million dollars behind him.

Suddenly, he realized that it wasn't the money, real or imagined, that had turned his life around. It was his newfound self-confidence that gave him the power to achieve anything he went after.

THE IMPORTANCE OF SELF-CONFIDENCE

All other things being equal, self-confidence is usually the single ingredient that determines whether a person is successful or unsuccessful.

Self-confidence is not something you are born with; it is acquired. Having self-confidence means you know what your talents are and believe that these talents will help you achieve your goals. It is having faith in your own abilities. It is how you feel about yourself.

To be an effective leader, self-confidence is even more important than talent, knowledge, and hard work. When you are confident, you are more likely to take action on your goals. The success of any undertaking starts when you believe in your ability at the start. In addition, leaders who are self-confident are willing to take calculated risks and do more than others might think is possible.

How you see yourself has an enormous impact on how others perceive you. When you are self-confident, you are more determined, better equipped to establish positive relationships, and more likely to achieve your goals. Self-confident leaders are usually more positive, and as a result, more fun to be around.

Your self-confidence is demonstrated in your behavior, your body language, how you look (demeanor), how you act, what you say, and how you say it. When you look, act, and sound confident, you will be confident. Since how you look, how you act, what you say, and how you say it are behaviors, self-confidence can be learned.

CAUSES OF LOW/NO SELF-CONFIDENCE

There are many reasons why individuals suffer from little or no self-confidence. Perhaps you were belittled as a child by your family, teachers, or friends for your looks, lack of athletic ability, or for some other reason. Perhaps you have had some serious set-backs financially, physically, mentally, or in one or more relationships. These experiences can also reduce your self-confidence. Perhaps, for whatever reason, you have fallen into the trap of using negative self-talk such as, "I'm not good at math," "I'm a poor reader, student, athlete, etc.;" "I'm not very coordinated." Focusing and dwelling on what you perceive to be negative traits or lack of ability only adds to low self-confidence and keeps you from achieving what you are capable of attaining.

These experiences can shake your self-confidence and lead you to believe that you are not worthy of success.

Many people are harder on themselves than they are on other people. We get down on ourselves for relatively small mistakes. We believe that other people are smarter than us, are better in some way, or are more confident. This trend can be damaging to our self-confidence and ability to develop our personal leadership.

INCREASING YOUR SELF-CONFIDENCE

You can learn to be more confident just as you learned to read, write, to drive a car, or anything else you've learned. To increase your self-confidence:

Look at your past accomplishments
Write down all the things you've accomplished thus far in your life. We take a lot of things for granted and overlook, or discount, many of the things we've accomplished, e.g. we've learned to walk, talk, ride a bicycle, drive a car, use a computer, and much, much more.

Look at your strengths
What do you do well? What do you have a passion for? What comes easy to you? Which of your talents gets the most attention from other people?

Know your limitations
Everyone has limitations. When you recognize an area that is holding you back, you can take positive action to overcome your limitation or in some way compensate for it.

Monitor your self-talk
Avoid negative self-talk by substituting positive self-talk. You are where you are and what you are because of the dominating thoughts that occupy your mind. Make sure you fill

your mind with words that will help you. Make a list of the positive things you want to be true about yourself and read your list on a regular basis – and especially after any set-back.

Be a life-long learner
Read books, attend seminars, workshops, or night school courses, listen to personal development CDs, and seek out people who are already skilled in the areas you want to improve.

Develop the habit of setting small goals and achieving them
Then, continue to set progressively more difficult goals. Each time you accomplish a goal, it puts a positive bump on your self-image and boosts your self-confidence.

Spend time with positive, supportive people
Notice the words they use, what they talk about, their posture, and other indicators of confidence. See what you can learn from these people. They were probably where you are confidence-wise at some point in their lives.

Learn to handle set-backs, defeats, and failures and put rejection in proper perspective
Most of the time people reject our proposals, not us as a person. Many times we boost our self-image more by bouncing back from these set-backs than we do from easy successes.

Maintain a presentable appearance, including appropriate attire and grooming
This will make you feel better about yourself, which will add to your attractiveness and improve your confidence.

Practice good posture
Stand and sit up straight, keep your chin up, and make eye contact.

Think positive
What you think on the inside will project on the outside.

Look for the best in others
Compliment them. Be positive. Avoid getting involved in gossip or complaining.

Maintain a high energy level by staying physically fit
Eat healthy foods, exercise, and get the proper amount of sleep, rest, and relaxation.

Make a list of your past and current accomplishments and add to it on a regular basis
Reflecting on past success will boost your confidence.

Make a list of your strengths and use affirmations and positive self-talk to encourage yourself
Put your list on a 3X5 card, in your daily planner, or on a small note pad you can review daily.

Smile
It will not only make you feel better about yourself, your smile will make others feel better about you. As you enter a room, begin a meeting, meet another person, or start any major activity, pause to smile. Oftentimes, a smile will be returned which will enhance your confidence.

Improve your skills and increase your knowledge
Learning something new and improving a skill are great self-confidence boosters.

Help someone else
When you help someone else, you momentarily take your mind off yourself and your troubles.

Face your fears
Acting with courage will give you the confidence to know that you can meet and conquer your challenges. Courage leads you to face adversities and endure their consequences. Facing your fears will give you valuable insight into how

to handle future adversities. Develop your courage and face your fears. Act as if it were impossible to fail.

Believe in yourself
Do not compare yourself to others. Instead, compare yourself to what you are capable of becoming. Your self-confidence will determine your level of success, how you deal with setbacks, and the goals you choose to accomplish.

Break larger goals and challenges into "bite-sized" chunks When you tackle and accomplish small goals and small challenges, you will ultimately achieve the larger goal or conquer the larger challenge. In the process, you will develop your courage and self-confidence and be better prepared to develop your personal leadership.

To quote Paul J. Meyer, "Confidence comes from experience. Experience comes from know-how. Know-how comes from having the courage to submit yourself to obstacles, situations, and circumstances where the average person shies away."

THE EIGHT P'S OF PERSONAL ACHIEVEMENT

Denis Waitley, author and motivational speaker, says, "Accept yourself as you are right now: an imperfect, changing, growing, and worthy person." No matter where you stand in your life right now, you are a worthy person – worthy of setting new and exciting goals - worthy of having more of the things you want out of life, worthy of developing and maintaining positive relationships, worthy of having your dream job or being in business for yourself, worthy of having a successful life."

Personal achievement will have a major impact on your self-confidence. To increase your personal achievement:

Plan Purposely

Another way of saying this is, "prior planning promotes professional performance." Most people spend more time planning a vacation than they do planning what they want to accomplish in other areas of their life, including their career. When you fail to plan, you plan to fail.

Prepare Properly

The Scout motto, "be prepared," is something everyone can heed. It's been said that luck is "preparation meeting opportunity." People who outperform their peers, excel in their career, achieve acclaim, and appear "lucky" have been better prepared.

Proceed Positively

You can plan purposely and prepare properly, but unless you take positive action, you will not enjoy the success you are capable of achieving.

Pursue Persistently

For small goals and easy accomplishments, planning purposely, preparing properly, and proceeding positively might be enough. However, for larger goals, more difficult tasks, and when obstacles and roadblocks get in your way, it is time for stronger measures. Persistence, or dogged determination, will help you break through hindering circumstances, past conditioning, obstacles, and roadblocks. Persistence will also help you get past the negative influence of what other people say, think, or do.

Paul J. Meyer said it best: "Whatever you vividly imagine, ardently desire, sincerely believe, and enthusiastically act upon, must inevitably come to pass."

INCREASING SELF-CONFIDENCE - SUMMARY

✓ Self-confidence is even more important than talent, knowledge, and hard work.

✓ Your self-confidence is demonstrated by how you look, how you act, what you say, and how you say it.

✓ Your self-confidence can be increased by being a life-long learner.

✓ How you see yourself has an enormous impact on how others perceive you.

✓ Focusing on improving one day at a time will build your self-confidence.

INCREASING SELF-CONFIDENCE - AFFIRMATIONS

✓ I have confidence in myself and my ability to succeed.

✓ I am committed to be a life-long learner.

✓ I use positive self-talk.

✓ I do something to improve some aspect of my life every day.

✓ I act with courage in difficult situations.

4.
Maintaining a High Energy Level

"Fatigue will make cowards of us all."

- Vince Lombardi

10 year-old Sarah was born with a muscle missing in her foot and wears a brace all the time. She went home one beautiful spring day to tell her dad she had competed in "field day" – that's where they have lots of races and other competitive events.

Because of her leg support, her dad tried to think of encouragement for Sarah, things he could say to her about not letting this get her down – but before he could say anything, she said, "Daddy, I won two of the races!" He couldn't believe it! And then Sarah said, "I had an advantage." Of course she did! She must have been given a head start…some kind of physical advantage. But again, before he could say anything, she said, "Daddy, I didn't get a head start…my advantage was I had to try harder!"

One thing that high achievers have in common is a high-energy level. They are able to persist until they reach their desired objective. They can overcome obstacles, hindering circumstances, set-backs, defeats, and other people's negativity.

THE CHOICE IS YOURS

At any given time, we all have a certain amount of energy available to us. How well we direct that energy will determine how productive we are. You can choose to direct your available energy in a positive, productive direction or diffuse it in a variety of directions, some of which could be counter-productive. The same amount of energy is there; it's how we choose to direct it that determines our results. How you use your energy can and needs to be a conscious choice.

Choose to have a positive attitude by focusing on what you can accomplish, not what you can't. Choose to have an attitude that generates energy in yourself and others, not one that drains energy from yourself and others.

Being fully engaged in work you enjoy generates energy. A high energy level will help you feel invigorated, confident, challenged, joyful, and connected. All of these characteristics will help you be the "generator" for others.

MAINTAINING A HIGH ENERGY LEVEL

Energy, not time, is the fundamental currency of high performance. Performance, health, and happiness are grounded in the skillful management of energy. The number of hours in a day is fixed, but the quantity and quality of energy available to us is not. It is our most precious resource.

Some things you can do to maintain a high-energy level include:

- Get the appropriate amount of sleep.

- Eat healthy; make sure you get a good balance of nutrients.

- Maintain a regular exercise program.

- Enjoy a hobby and/or other recreational pursuits.

- Do stretching and deep breathing exercises to keep a good flow of oxygen in your muscles.

- Set aside personal time with family and close

friends.

■ Help someone who is less fortunate than you.

■ Reflect on your past accomplishments and victories.

■ Maintain a regular program of reading or listening to positive books and CDs.

INCREASING ENERGY THROUGH LEARNING

Most people are energized by learning. One method of learning is reading. However, the average American reads less than one book a year. Organizing book studies is a great way to increase energy by creating a learning environment.

To get started, choose a book, article, pamphlet, CD, or other material. Be sure to pick something that has group appeal and application to work skills and success. Once you have selected your material, agree on a weekly study schedule and assign the first week's reading, or if weekly is not appropriate for your organization, meet twice a month or monthly.

For best results, meet at a scheduled time for a predetermined amount of time. When everyone does the appropriate reading, these meetings do not need to take a lot of time. In small groups, fifteen to thirty minutes gives everyone two to three minutes to share their ideas and how they will apply them. Appoint a timekeeper, if necessary, to keep the meeting on schedule.

During the meetings, have one team member be responsible for leading the review and discussion. The emphasis needs to be on how the material applies to work or life. Have team members choose one insight they can apply in the coming week as they also prepare to cover the next study assignment. Before ending the meeting, choose the next week's review and discussion leader.

ENERGIZING OTHERS

In the fall when you see geese heading south for the winter flying along in the "V" formation, you might be interested in knowing what science has discovered about why they fly that way.

It has been learned that as each bird flaps its wings, it creates uplift for the bird immediately following. By flying in a "V" formation, the whole flock adds at least 71% greater flying range than if each bird flew on its own. Quite similar to people who are part of a team and share a common direction get where they are going quicker and easier, because they are traveling on the trust of one another and lift each other up along the way.

Whenever a goose falls out of formation, it suddenly feels the drag and resistance of trying to go through it alone and quickly gets back into formation to take advantage of the power of the flock. If we have as much sense as a Goose, we will stay in formation and share information with those who are headed the same way that we are going.

When the lead goose gets tired, he rotates back in the wing and another goose takes over. It pays to share leadership and take turns doing hard jobs.

The geese honk from behind to encourage those up front to keep their speed. Words of support and inspiration help energize those on the front line, helping them to keep pace in spite of the day-to-day pressures and fatigue. It is important that our honking be encouraging. Otherwise it's just - well, honking!

Finally, when a goose gets sick or is wounded by a gunshot and falls out, two geese fall out of the formation and follow the injured one down to help and protect him. They stay with him until he is either able to fly or until he is dead, and then they launch out with another formation to catch up with their group. When one of us is down, it's up to the others to stand by us in our time of trouble. If we have the sense of a goose, we will stand by each other when things get rough. We will stay in formation with those headed where we want to go.

As a leader, your energy affects the energy of those around you. Use the following ideas to energize those around you:

Say what you will do and do what you say.
When people know you are a person of integrity and they can count on you, their trust level goes up, and they can use their energy in productive pursuits.

Help others remember their past successes
People have a tendency to vividly remember their past mistakes and failures and to forget or diminish their past successes. By helping them remember their past successes, you help boost their energy.

Help others set short-term goals and break more complex goals into "bite-sized," achievable chunks
When people enjoy frequent successes, they become energized.   Success breeds success is absolutely true.   Small successes lead to bigger successes.

Look for opportunities to recognize and praise others
Praise is a great elixir. It builds self-esteem, bolsters self-image, and creates an adrenalin rush that generates an abundance of energy. Praise is the catalyst for energy. Affirm team members' efforts to keep them from getting discouraged.

Help others focus on the next step
When people realize the power of progressive realization and develop an "I can do that (next step)" attitude, improved performance and success are inevitable.

Help others identify their passion

Passion creates energy. When people know what their passion is and take steps to pursue and fulfill it, they are going to be energized. You can help them identify their passion by asking them questions about what is important to them, by watching what they pay attention to, and by observing and giving them feedback on how they spend their time.

Inspect what you expect

People respect you more when you inspect what you expect. This helps people become more accountable, and being accountable produces energy.

Keep score

Keeping score helps people know whether they are winning or losing and stamps out uncertainty. Knowing that you are winning or losing generates energy. Uncertainty drains energy. Do what you can to stamp out uncertainty.

Encourage others

When people feel encouraged, they can overcome incredible adversity. Overcoming adversity builds self-esteem and generates more energy. Help team members look for solutions. Worrying about negative issues uses energy in a nonproductive way.

Help others bring out their enthusiasm

If people are not naturally enthusiastic, get them to act enthusiastically. Enthusiasm radiates, is contagious, and sells. It gives people energy and creates a positive aura that helps people relax and feel confident.

MAINTAINING A HIGH ENERGY LEVEL - SUMMARY

✓   How you choose to use your energy will determine how productive you are.

✓ Engaging in work you enjoy generates energy.

✓ Most people are energized by learning.

✓ The energy you have as a leader affects the energy level of those around you.

✓ Helping others is a great way to boost your own energy level, as well as the energy level of the person you are helping.

MAINTAINING A HIGH ENERGY LEVEL - AFFIRMATIONS

✓ I choose to direct my energy in a positive way.

✓ I get the appropriate amount of sleep and eat healthy in order to maintain a high energy level.

✓ I am committed to learning new things through increased reading time.

✓ I look for ways to encourage and praise others.

✓ I say what I will do and do what I say.

5.
Accepting Personal Responsibility

"You must take personal responsibility. You cannot change the circumstances, the seasons, or the wind, but you can change yourself. That is something you have charge of."

- Jim Rohn

An elderly carpenter was ready to retire. He told his employer-contractor of his plans to leave the house building business to live a more leisurely life with his wife and enjoy his extended family. He would miss the paycheck each week, but he wanted to retire. They could get by.

The contractor was sorry to see his good worker go & asked if he could build just one more house as a personal favor. The carpenter said yes, but over time it was easy to see that his heart was not in his work. He resorted to shoddy workmanship and used inferior materials. It was an unfortunate way to end a dedicated career.

When the carpenter finished his work, his employer came to inspect the house. Then he handed the front door key to the carpenter and said, "This is your house... my gift to you."

The carpenter was shocked!

What a shame! If he had only known he was building his own house, he would have done it all so differently.

So it is with us. We build our lives, a day at a time, often putting less than our best into the building. Then, with a shock, we realize we have to live in the house we have built. If we could do it over, we would do it much differently.

But, you cannot go back. You are the carpenter, and every day you hammer a nail, place a board, or erect a wall. Someone once said, "Life is a do-it-yourself project." Your attitude, and the choices you make today, help build the "house" you will live in tomorrow. Therefore, build wisely!

ACCEPTING PERSONAL RESPONSIBILITY

When it comes right down to it, there is only one person responsible for your life – YOU. Others can influence you, support you, or even help you, but you are ultimately responsible. You have total control over your thoughts and actions; thus, you are responsible for how you think and how you act. In addition, you are responsible for your own knowledge. Regardless of the quantity or quality of your formal education, you can learn what you need to be successful through books, recordings, seminars, the Internet, and many other sources.

To accept personal responsibility and achieve more of what you want out of your career and life:

1. Have a written and specific goals program - both personal and business

When you know where you stand, where you want to go, and how you're going to get there, you will have more confidence and be more motivated to achieve your goals. Since writing crystallizes thought, and crystallized thought motivates action, it is important that your goals are in writing.

2. Take initiative

Getting started is critical to your success, so don't wait for someone else to get going. Someone once said, "Well-started is half-done."

3. Be self-reliant

Once you get started, keep going. Two of my favorite sayings that support this point are: "Winners never quit and quitters never win," and "It is always too soon to quit."

4. Choose your reaction

There will always be obstacles to any worthwhile goal. The way you respond to these obstacles, and the choices you make as a result of them, will determine the magnitude of your success. Remember, it's not your situation that affects the outcome; it's your reaction to the situation.

5. Prepare yourself

A commitment to continuous growth is essential in the pursuit and achievement of worthwhile goals. You'll be no better off tomorrow than you are today, except for the books you read, the messages you listen to, and the people you associate with. If you want to have more, you need to be more.

6. Believe in yourself

Make a list of your personal strengths and past accomplishments. Review your lists and add to them on a regular basis. By focusing on your strengths instead of your weaknesses and on your accomplishments instead of your problems, you will bolster your belief in yourself, helping you break through obstacles, road blocks, and other hindering circumstances.

7. Visualize your success

"Objects in mirror are closer than they appear" is etched in every automobile's passenger side mirror. The same is true when you visualize your goals. Your goals will be accomplished in less time when you visualize them as already completed. Put symbols of your future accomplishments on your bathroom mirror. You will soon discover that these accomplishments are closer than you thought.

8. Establish and maintain positive relationships

We usually need other people to help us reach our goals, whether it's in a support role or direct assistance. Establishing, maintaining, and nurturing relationships will pay big dividends.

9. Take appropriate risks

Achieving worthwhile goals requires taking a risk in the form of extra effort, persistence, determination, an "I will not be denied" attitude, and a "whatever it takes" attitude.

10. Expand your resources.

Unless your goal is highly personal, you can usually get other people to help you achieve it, so enlist family members, friends, or business associates.

11. Be "on fire" about your goals

When you're excited about your goals and enthusiastic about the outcome, you'll draw on inner resources that will help your goals become reality.

12. Commit to greatness

To achieve great goals, you need to be the best you that you're capable of becoming. You need to make your life extraordinary by developing and using more of your talents and abilities.

IF IT IS TO BE, IT IS UP TO ME

Personal responsibility is about accepting the consequences of your actions and having the integrity to honor your commitments to yourself and others.

Unfulfilled commitments, shirking your responsibilities, or blaming others, and/or circumstances, for your results drains your psychic energy. On the other hand, completion of your commitments and accepting personal responsibility restores your energy. Even though you do not have complete control over your results, you do have control over your behaviors, actions (or inactions), and attitude.

President Harry S. Truman had a sign on his desk that stated, "The buck stops here." Just like the former President, you need to be responsible for your actions. Your sign could read, "If it's to be, it's up to me."

When you don't get the results you want and need, it is important to accept personal responsibility and change your behaviors, actions, and/or attitude. Doing this consistently will improve your performance and results.

To accept personal responsibility, believe in yourself, your dreams, and your ability to pursue them. Know where you stand now and where you want to go. Then, you can use this information to develop a plan for how you're going to get there.

ACCEPTING PERSONAL RESPONSIBILITY - SUMMARY

✓ You are the only person responsible for your life.

✓ You have total control over your thoughts and actions.

✓ It's not your situation that affects the outcome; it's your reaction to the situation.

✓ A commitment to continuous growth is essential in the pursuit and achievement of worthwhile goals.

✓ Completion of your commitments and accepting personal responsibility restores your energy.

ACCEPTING PERSONAL RESPONSIBILITY- AFFIRMATIONS

✓ I accept personal responsibility.

✓ I have written and specific goals.

✓ I take initiative.

✓ I establish, nurture, and maintain relationships.

✓ I believe in myself.

Part II
Self-Motivated

....

Once thought to be external, motivation is now clearly understood to be generated internally. Motivation is your drive, your get-up-and-go. It is your desire to be more, to do more, and to achieve more. Motivation is developed within yourself.

Self-motivation is a crucial component of personal leadership. Without it, you will plan less, do less, and achieve less. Without self-motivation, you will rely on others to offer up encouragement and praise, and you will wait on others for personal progress.

If you want to make things happen, you must be self-motivated. Motivation effects action. Without action, you cannot progress toward your goals. You remain stagnant. However, with motivation, you can excel. You can set gaols and meet them. You can become what you want to be.

Self-motivated individuals are inspiring. Their behaviors are admirable, and their positive attitude is contagious. Self-motivated individuals draw others toward them and, as a result, self-motivated individuals become leaders.

Throughout the next three chapters, you will identify your preferred communication style and learn how you can use it to motivate yourself and others. You will explore the relationship between desire and motivation and learn how to get in and work in your ZONE. Finally, you will learn how self-motivation will enable you to persevere through any difficulties you will face while on your leadership journey. Read on to be inspired!

6.

Understanding Yourself and Those You Lead

"Before you can understand, motivate, and lead others, you first must be able to understand, motivate, and lead yourself."

- Paul J. Meyer

An old hill farming crofter trudges several miles through freezing snow to his local and very remote chapel for Sunday service. No one else is there, aside from the clergyman.

"I'm not sure it's worth proceeding with the service - might we do better to go back to our warm homes and a hot drink?.." asks the clergyman, inviting a mutually helpful reaction from his audience of one.

"Well, I'm just a simple farmer," says the old crofter, "But when I go to feed my herd, and if only one beast turns up, I sure don't leave it hungry."

So the clergyman, feeling somewhat ashamed, delivers his service - all the bells and whistles, hymns and readings, lasting a good couple of hours - finishing proudly with the fresh observation that no matter how small the need, our duty remains. And he thanks the old farmer for the lesson he has learned.

"Was that okay?" asks the clergyman, as the two set off home.

"Well I'm just a simple farmer," says the old crofter, "But when I go to feed my herd, and if only one beast turns up,

I sure don't force it to eat what I brought for the whole herd..."

As individuals, we all have preferences or tendencies for how we communicate with others. In addition, we all have different ways in which we interpret communication. Consequently, it is essential that we are able to recognize and understand our preferred communication as both the sender and the receiver of the message.

Most individuals use a combination of several different styles, depending on both the person to whom they are speaking and the situation or topic being discussed.

There are essentially four different communication styles, and each of us has the ability to choose which style we will use. Although we have a preferred style that we will typically fall back on, we can and should adapt our style to accommodate the preferred style of the individual we are communicating with.

Self-awareness plays a significant role in effective communication. Understanding your own communication style will help you create a lasting impression on others by properly adapting your style to the style of the individual you are communicating with.

Understanding your own communication style is the first step to becoming a good communicator. Secondly, you must recognize that individuals have different communication styles, and that it is your responsibility as a good communicator to accommodate their needs.

No communication style is superior or inferior to another. The combination of all four styles are vital to productivity. As a result, you should learn to appreciate the contributions that each style makes to overall success.

Platinum Rule: Treat others how they want to be treated.

A good communicator understands and appreciates

all styles and is flexible enough to modify their own style to meet the needs of the individual they are communicating with.   The four communication styles are:

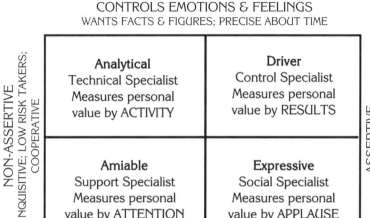

CONTROLS EMOTIONS & FEELINGS
WANTS FACTS & FIGURES; PRECISE ABOUT TIME

Analytical Technical Specialist Measures personal value by ACTIVITY	**Driver** Control Specialist Measures personal value by RESULTS	
Amiable Support Specialist Measures personal value by ATTENTION	**Expressive** Social Specialist Measures personal value by APPLAUSE	

NON-ASSERTIVE
INQUISITIVE; LOW RISK TAKERS; COOPERATIVE

ASSERTIVE
DIRECTIVE; HIGH RISK TAKERS; COMPETITIVE

RESPONSIVE
EXPRESSIVE ABOUT FEELINGS; PEOPLE-ORIENTED; SUBJECTIVE

IDENTIFYING STYLES

Once you know your own communication style, you will want to determine the preferred communication style of the individual you communicate with.   You can do this quickly by asking yourself a few questions.

First, ask yourself how RESPONSIVE the person is. Determine if the individual:

• Is animated or reserved.

• Acts eager or cautious.

• Has little interest in facts or wants all the facts.

• Openly shares feelings or limits feelings.

Next, ask yourself how ASSERTIVE the person is? Does the individual:

• Make statements or ask questions?

• Express himself aggressively and dominantly or quiet and submissive?

• Tend to lean forward or back?

If the person is assertive and tends to control his or her emotions and feelings, this person has Driver tendencies.

If the person is assertive and tends to be responsive, this person has Expressive tendencies.

If the person is non-assertive and tends to be responsive, this person has Amiable tendencies.

If the person is non-assertive and tends to control his or her feelings and emotions, this person has Analytical tendencies.

Keep in mind that people have a blend of all the quadrants. They can draw on the tendencies of their non-predominant quadrant as needed. Likewise, you can and should flex your natural communication style to appeal to the other person's natural style. The better you get at reading other people's tendencies and adapting your own style to meet their needs, the more effective you'll be at communicating with them.

UNDERSTANDING THE FOUR STYLES

Recognizing an individual's preferred communication style is only the first step. Understanding each of the four styles will enable you to become a better communicator.

Driver:

Determined	Factual	Impersonal	Intense
Pushy	Demanding	Efficient	Forceful
Harsh	Decisive	Self-Reliant	Dominant
Impatient			

Expressive:

Stimulating	Personable	Excitable	Manipulative
Animated	Undisciplined	Enthusiastic	Intuitive
Outgoing	Unstructured	Dramatic	Creative
Inspiring	Persuasive		

Amiable:

Supportive	Considerate	Willing	Careful
Agreeable	Quiet	Cooperative	Obliging
Warm	Dependable	Contented	Reliable
Patient	Excellent listener		

Analytical:

Exacting	Conservative	Orderly	Logical
Precise	Systematic	Persistent	Punctual
Critical	Indecisive	Formal	Serious
Industrious	Organized	Thorough	

RELATING TO OTHER STYLES

Once you have identified and understand your own communication style, it is essential that you are able to identify the style of the individual you are communicating with. Modifying your own communication style to meet the needs of the other individual is called style flexing and is a key element of becoming a good communicator.

I. **Driver - Direct & Decisive; like challenges, taking action, & getting results.**

» Be direct, straightforward, and open to their need for results.

» Make communication brief and to the point.

» Respect their need for autonomy.

» Be clear about rules and expectations.

» Let them initiate.

» Show your competence.

» Stick to the topic.

» Show independence.

» Eliminate time wasters.

» Be prepared for lack of empathy, sensitivity, and little social interaction.

II. **Expressive - Optimistic & Outgoing; "people" people, like participating on teams, sharing ideas, and energizing & entertaining others.**

» Be friendly, emotionally honest, and recognize their contributions.

» Approach them informally.

» Be relaxed and sociable.

» Let them verbalize thoughts and feelings.

» Keep the conversation light.

» Provide written details.

» Give public recognition for individual accomplishments.

» Use humor.

» Be prepared for attempts to persuade and influence others, need for "lime light", over-estimating self and others, over-selling ideas, and vulnerability to perceived rejection.

III. Amiable - Cooperative & Sympathetic; helpful, like working behind the scenes, work in a consistent, predictable manner, and good listeners.

» Be relaxed, agreeable, cooperative, and show appreciation.

» Be logical and systematic in your approach.

» Provide a consistent and secure environment.

» Let them know how things will be done.

» Use sincere appreciation.

» Show their importance to the organization.

» Let them move slowly into change.

» Be prepared for friendly approach, resistance to change, difficulty prioritizing, and difficulty with deadlines.

IV. Analytical: Concerned & Correct; sticklers for quality; plan ahead; employ systematic approaches; check and re-check for accuracy.

» Minimize socializing, give details, and value accuracy.

» Give clear expectations.

» Show dependability.

» Show loyalty.

» Be tactful and emotionally reserved.

» Allow precedent to be a guide.

» Be precise and stay focused.

» Value high standards.

» Be prepared for discomfort with ambiguity, resistance to vague or general information, desire to double check, and little need to affiliate with people.

STRENGTHENING YOUR RELATIONSHIPS

Good communication will help strengthen your relationships with others since they will begin to feel heard, understood, and important. Remember to style flex your own style to meet the needs of the other individual.

When working with Drivers, focus on their goals, be punctual and organized, use their time wisely, and don't challenge them. Be efficient. Support their conclusions and actions. Stick to business. Provide options and probabilities. Help them save time. Give benefits that answer WHAT.

Start with big picture when communicating with Expressives. Use testimonials. Make them look good. Don't deal in details. Help them save effort. Be stimulating. Support their dreams and intuitions. Give benefits that answer WHO.

When communicating with Amiables, work to understand them personally, build a step-by-step relationship, keep change to a minimum, and minimize their risk. Take time to be agreeable. Support their relationships and feelings. Give benefits that answer WHY.

Analyticals require facts/data. When communicating, be accurate, stick to business, be persistent, and put it in writing with pros and cons. Help them by letting them save face. Take time to be accurate. Support their principles and thinking. Give benefits that answer HOW.

UNDERSTANDING YOURSELF
AND THOSE YOU LEAD -
SUMMARY

✓ We all have a preferred communication style.

✓ No communication style is superior or inferior to another.

✓ Effective communication requires you to communicate with others how they want to be communicated with.

✓ There are four different communication styles; Driver, Expressive, Amiable, and Analytical.

✓ Good communication skills will help strengthen your relationships with others.

UNDERSTANDING YOURSELF
AND THOSE YOU LEAD -
AFFIRMATIONS

✓ I understand my own communication style.

✓ I style flex to meet the needs of the person I am communicating with.

✓ I appreciate the contributions that each style has on effective communication.

✓ I listen to others to help them feel important and understood.

✓ I am committed to becoming a better communicator.

7.
Achieving a High Level of Self-Motivation

"The starting point of all achievement is desire. Keep this constantly in mind. Weak desire brings weak results, just as a small amount of fire makes a small amount of heat."

-Napoleon Hill

There once was an eager student who wanted to gain wisdom and insight. He went to the wisest of the town, Socrates, to seek his counsel. Socrates was an old soul and had great knowledge of many things. The boy asked the town sage how he too could acquire such mastery. Being a man of few words, Socrates chose not to speak, but to illustrate.

He took the child to the beach and, with all of his clothes still on, walked straight out into the water. He loved to do curious things like that, especially when he was trying to prove a point. The pupil gingerly followed his instruction and walked into the sea, joining Socrates where the water was just below their chins. Without saying a word, Socrates reached out and put his hands on the boy's shoulders. Looking deep into his student's eyes, Socrates pushed the student's head under the water with all his might.

A struggle ensued and just before a life was taken away, Socrates released his captive. The boy raced to the surface and, gasping for air and choking from the salt water, looked around for Socrates in order to seek his retaliation on the sage. To the student's bewilderment, the old man was already patiently waiting on the beach.

When the student arrived on the sand, he angrily shouted, "Why did you try to kill me?"

The wise man calmly retorted with a question, "When you were underneath the water, not sure if you would live to see another day, what did you want more than anything in the world?"

The student took a few moments to reflect, then went with his intuition. Softly, he said, "I wanted to breathe."

Socrates, now illuminated by his own huge smile, looked at the boy comfortingly and said, "Ah! When you want wisdom and insight as badly as you wanted to breathe, it is then that you shall have it."

ALL MOTIVATION IS SELF-MOTIVATION

One of the characteristics of a successful person is self-motivation. Consequently, to develop your personal leadership, you need to be self-motivated and must "wind your own clock." Self-motivation comes from desire; the stronger your desire, the stronger your self-motivation.

Motivation can be described as a "motive" for "action". A motive is a reason, purpose, or goal for doing something – for taking action. Taking action is the go, do, or act. Action is our behavior.

Motivation Balance Beam

Motive	Action
Reason	Go
Purpose	Do
Goal	Act

MOTIVeAcTION

If we substitute the word "benefit" for motive and "cost" for action, for motivation to occur, the benefit has to outweigh the cost. When the benefit is only equal to the cost, or less than the cost, motivation does not exist.

When you set a goal and start working toward it, you are motivated. By focusing on your motive, reason, purpose, and/or goal, and by diminishing the action or cost (in time, money, energy, and emotion), you are more likely to be self-motivated. You will want to take the necessary actions because you can see the personal benefit.

In the truest sense, you cannot motivate another person; you can only create an environment in which they can motivate themselves. Consequently, it is imperative that you create an environment that will enable you to motivate yourself.

In general, people are motivated to gain a benefit or avoid a loss. Gaining a benefit can mean different things for different people, but in most cases, it can be categorized as a benefit in the areas of pride, profit, or pleasure. Pride in this sense means taking pleasure or satisfaction in an achievement or possession. Profit can mean money or some other form of personal gain. Pleasure is something we enjoy or have fun doing or having.

Avoiding a loss and preventing pain are synonymous. We might avoid getting our feelings hurt or doing something stupid. We will avoid things that will cause us physical pain. We fear losing our loved ones or material possessions.

When you examine why you behave the way you do, chances are one of the four P's – pride, profit, pleasure, and pain – is at play.

There are several different types of motivation. Fear motivation is based on force, and at best, only gains compliance. Fear motivation is temporary because it is external.

Similarly, incentive motivation is also temporary because it is external. Incentive motivation is based on reward and usually requires giving more and more for less and less.

The only kind of lasting motivation is attitude motivation, which is based on change. Attitude motivation affects how you react to others and how others react to you. It is permanent because it is internal. You take action because you want to not because you think you have to, and action is an essential component of flaming your desire.

FLAMING YOUR DESIRE

Desire can be defined as a strong intention or aim. When you have a desire, it means you are capable of fulfilling it. You can be what you want to be.

Fortunately, desire can be developed. The amount of desire you develop is up to you. With a sufficient amount of desire, you can accomplish almost anything.

Desire is the emotion that causes individuals to sacrifice, make an extra effort, go the extra mile, overcome obstacles, and follow through on tasks, projects, and goals to completion. In order to develop your desire, focus on your goals, accomplishments, and what you can do rather than what you cannot do. You must visualize and affirm your success.

HOW TO DEVELOP YOUR DESIRE

Just as flaming a smoldering log will make it glow red-hot, you can flame your desire by identifying goals that are important to you, identifying what you are passionate about, what your talents are, and what you value most. In addition:

Focus on your goals.
Someone defined a problem as what happens when you take your eyes off your goals. When you know where you stand, where you want to go, and how you're going to get there, your desire will help you achieve your goals.

Identify your passion.
What causes you to get up each morning? What causes time to fly by? What do you enjoy doing more than anything else?

Learn to overcome obstacles.
Just as lifting weights will build your muscles, overcoming obstacles will help you develop your leadership ability. Everyone faces obstacles, and the better you get at facing and overcoming them, the better prepared you'll be to handle more difficult challenges.

Be willing to pay the price.
All action has a price – in time, money, energy, effort, or emotion. When you are committed to your goals and a successful life and you're willing to pay the price, your desire will help propel you toward success.

THE IMPORTANCE OF ENTHUSIASM

Enthusiasm is a zest for or an extreme interest in a subject, cause, or life itself. It is more than excitement or inspiration.

When I was 36, I was invited to watch one of my neighbors play in the finals of the club championship at a local tennis club. Watching my neighbor play at a highly competitive level caused me to become curious about playing tennis, which, in turn, led me to take an interest in tennis as a hobby. I learned as much as I could about tennis through reading books, listening to recordings on tennis, subscribing to Ten-

nis magazine, watching matches, taking lessons, and lining up practice matches. I became enthusiastic about tennis.

As I improved as a tennis player, I started to believe that I could play competitively. My enthusiasm led me to play tennis competitively for over 25 years. As a result, I maintained good physical health and made a lot of great friends. My success in tennis boosted my self-esteem which, in turn, helped me become more successful in business and other areas of my life.

Enthusiasm usually starts with curiosity. When you are curious about something, you naturally take an interest in it. As a result, you gain knowledge about it. Finally, when you develop belief in what you became curious about, your enthusiasm will blossom.

Fortunately, enthusiasm is learned. If you are not naturally enthusiastic, get started by acting enthusiastic. Enthusiasm gives you energy and communicates that you are happy and successful. It creates a positive aura and helps you relax and feel confident. In addition, enthusiasm… DOESN'T COST ANYTHING.

GETTING INTO YOUR ZONE

Self-motivated individuals spend a lot of time working in their zone. The phrase "in a zone" usually refers to a situation where someone is performing in an extraordinary manner.

People can be described as being in their ZONE when they appear to be working effortlessly and getting optimum results. When a task or job challenges a person's abilities, the opportunity to be in the ZONE exists. When challenge is low and ability is high, the person may become bored, distracted, and have a tendency to be sloppy or make mistakes. When a challenge is above a person's skill level, it can cause stress, frustration, and tension, which leads to poor performance.

You cannot be in the ZONE all the time. However, you can improve the odds of being in your ZONE by matching jobs, challenges, and goals to your skill level. You can also get into your ZONE by increasing your skill level.

Getting Into Your Zone

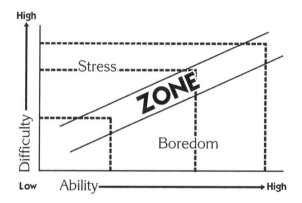

When you work in your ZONE, you are more productive, feel happier, use less energy, get better results, and are easier to coach. Here are some steps you can take to multiply the amount of time you spend in your ZONE:

- Spend as much time as possible in your areas of strength. You perform better when you work in your areas of strength because you feel more comfortable.

- Make sure you know what your goals are, what behaviors are necessary to achieve them, and what successful results look like.

- Be aware of and celebrate your progress.

You can probably remember times when you were in a zone. You were operating at maximum effectiveness with a minimum amount of energy. You lost all track of time. You accomplished more than you ever dreamed possible. You were excited.

Simply put, you are in a zone when your abilities match your challenges. The bigger the challenges, the bigger your abilities need to be. Likewise, if you have tremendous ability, you need to get in situations where you have tremendous challenges and opportunities.

Here are some things you can do to get into your zone and stay there most of the time:

Have a written and specific goals program.
Written goals are important because writing crystallizes thought, and crystallized thought motivates action. Your goals program needs to include goals in every area of your life, including career, family, financial, mental, physical, social, and spiritual. Having goals in every area of your life will give you balance, and you'll use more of your potential.

Develop and protect your attitude.
It's easy to get swept up into the environment and influence of negative people. To offset this tendency, you can listen to positive CDs, read positive books, and use visualization to push out the negative thoughts that creep into your conscious and subconscious mind.

Use leverage.
You can gain leverage through the influence of other people. Tap into their influence, credibility, and knowledge to help you reach your goals. You can develop leverage by becoming an expert in your chosen field; be a specialist rather than a generalist. You can also use systems and scripts that allow you to replicate your best efforts with the least amount of energy.

Be persistent.
Ninety percent of all failure comes from quitting too soon.

When you're focused on a goal that's important to you and you encounter obstacles, do whatever it takes to go over, under, around, or through the obstacles.

Embrace continuous improvement.

One of my favorite examples of embracing continuous improvement involves the 10 year-old daughter of my long-time tennis partner. She was playing first base on a girls' softball team. In a game where her team was getting defeated soundly, she was called in to pitch, even though it wasn't normal in that league for 10 year-olds to pitch. The coach had used all of his 11 and 12 year-old pitchers to no avail. After she took a few warm-up pitches, she faced her first batter. Her first three pitches were not even close to the strike zone. At that point, she walked off the mound and headed toward the dugout. My first reaction was that she was discouraged and wanted the coach to take her out. Instead, she stopped at the first base line and said to the coach in a loud voice, "What can I do to improve?" The coach gave her a few tips, she applied them, and her results improved dramatically.

When was the last time you asked yourself, "What can I do to improve?" When was the last time you asked your business coach or mentor, "What can I do to improve?"

When you have a written and specific goals program, a positive mental attitude, leverage, persistence, take daily action on your goals, and constantly look for ways to improve, you'll be operating in your zone a high percentage of the time.

Self-motivation is a key component when developing personal leadership. In addition, self-motivated individuals are more likely to succeed. When we refer to success or a successful life, we define success as the pursuit of a worthy goal or ideal. This definition means that the success is in the pursuit and is a journey, not a destination. As a result, when you set a goal and start pursuing it, or when you pursue a worthy ideal, the moment you start – you are successful.

ACHIEVING A HIGH LEVEL OF SELF-MOTIVATION - SUMMARY

✓ Desire drives motivation. The higher your desire, the more self-motivated you become.

✓ It is your responsibility to create an environment in which you can be self-motivated.

✓ Attitude motivation is based on change and is the only form on lasting motivation.

✓ Enthusiasm gives you energy and is an important component of becoming self-motivated.

✓ Self-motivated individuals spend a lot of time working in their zone.

ACHIEVING A HIGH LEVEL OF SELF-MOTIVATION - AFFIRMATIONS

✓ I am a self-motivated individual.

✓ I set goals in order to flame my desire and promote self-motivation.

✓ I promote a positive aura by acting enthusiastically.

✓ I avoid negative people and situations.

✓ I spend as much time working in my zone as possible.

8.

Keeping on with Perseverance

"That which we persist in doing becomes easier – not that the nature of the task has changed, but our ability to do it has increased."

- Emerson

Two frogs fell into a vat of cream. They tried to get out by climbing up the side of the vat, but it was too slippery and steep. There was no solid ground with which to hop out. Each time, they slipped back again.

Finally, one frog said to the other, "We'll never get out of here. I give up." So down he went and eventually drowned.

The other frog decided to keep trying and kept kicking and kicking, hoping he would get his footing and be able to hop out.

Eventually the constant kicking turned the cream into butter, and so with one final effort, the frog leaped out.

PERSISTENCE, DETERMINATION, AND PERSEVERANCE

Persistence, determination, and perseverance are all closely related and are key to developing personal leadership.

Persistence is holding on to something important and not letting go, despite hindering circumstances.

Determination can be defined as firmness of purpose; resolve. Perseverance is commitment, hard work, patience, and endurance.

Perseverance is being able to handle difficulties calmly and without complaint. Perseverance is trying again and again until you succeed.

Helen Keller said, "We can do anything we want to if we stick to it long enough." There are many great examples of individuals who persevered despite handicaps and disabilities:

- Beethoven (composer) - was deaf
- Ray Charles (musician) - was blind
- Thomas Edison (inventor) - had a learning problem
- Albert Einstein (scientist) - had a learning disability
- Stevie Wonder (musician) - is blind
- James Earl Jones (actor) - was a stutterer
- Helen Keller (author) - was deaf and blind
- Marlee Matlin (actress) - is deaf
- Franklin D. Roosevelt (president) - was paralyzed from polio
- Vincent Van Gogh (artist) - was mentally ill
- Itzhak Perlman (concert violinist) - was paralyzed from the waist down
- Stephen Hawking (physicist) - has Lou Gehrig's disease

These individuals personify the adage, "It's not our situation; it's our reaction to our situation that really counts."

OVERCOMING ADVERSITY

Adversity is unavoidable. There will be family issues, financial issues, health issues, or relationship issues that create roadblocks to your goals. Consequently, overcoming adversity is a necessary part of developing personal leadership and is essential to developing your perseverance.

It is important to deal with adversity in the moment.

Don't worry about the past or be too concerned about the future. Handle the present adversity by using your energy to remove or go around the obstacle rather than trying to place blame or be frozen in fear about the future. Keep your adversity in perspective. Chances are there have been people who have experienced worse situations than you are in and have successfully overcome them. You can too.

Adversity helps us grow. When we set a goal and nothing gets in our way, we will achieve the goal in the exact proportion that we set originally. When there are obstacles and roadblocks to our goals, we grow when we figure out ways to overcome or get around these obstacles. Just as our muscles grow when we lift weights or exercise, our achievement "muscles" will grow when we overcome the adversities that face us. Sometimes we just need to push ourselves a little further to understand what we are really capable of doing.

When faced with a roadblock, we have a choice; we can either go over, under, around, or through the roadblock, or we can give up on our goals and return to our former life. The choice is ours to make.

Did you know that an eagle knows when a storm is approaching long before it breaks?

The eagle will fly to some high spot and wait for the winds to come. When the storm hits, it sets its wings so that the wind will pick it up and lift it above the storm. While the storm rages below, the eagle is soaring above it.

The eagle does not escape the storm. It simply uses the storm to lift it higher. It rises on the winds that bring the storm.

When the storms of life come upon us - and all of us will experience them - we can rise above them by setting our minds and our belief toward God. The storms do not have to overcome us. We can allow God's power to lift us above them.

God enables us to ride the winds of the storm that bring sickness, tragedy, failure, and disappointment in our lives. We can soar above the storm.

Remember, it is not the burdens of life that weigh us down, it is how we handle them.

Developing your determination by overcoming adversity will help you persevere through hardships and other types of set-backs. Here are some steps you can take to develop your determination and achieve more of your goals:

- When you catch yourself having a "pity party" or otherwise feeling sorry for yourself, replace negative thoughts with positive thoughts and take some short-range, physical action that will bust you out of your funk and start you on the path to the achievement of your goals.

- Refocus on your purpose and goals.

- Do something for someone else. This will make you feel better about yourself, help you forget your challenges temporarily, and strengthen your determination to help yourself.

- When you get stuck or start to get discouraged, take a break or exercise, even if it's just doing some stretching exercises where you are. This mental and physical break can help renew your determination.

- Avoid getting sidetracked by less important things. Turn off the TV. Avoid surfing the Web. Focus your attention on your goals. The reason water comes through the nozzle of a garden hose or fire hose with such force is because the nozzle restricts the water to one opening. You need to do the same thing when you are working on an important goal or project.

FOCUS ON STRENGTHS

From early childhood, we are conditioned to "fix" our weaknesses. When adults are asked to list their strengths, most of the time it is a struggle for them to list more than a few. When those same adults are asked to list their weaknesses, a much longer list is usually forthcoming.

Most adults have been exposed to numerous people in positions of authority who were determined to help them fix what was wrong with them. In other words, fix their weaknesses. It is a myth to think that fixing weaknesses makes everything better. The best way to drive excellence is to focus on strengths and manage weaknesses.

To focus on strengths, determine your areas of strength and find ways to spend more time in these areas and less time in your areas of weakness. When working in your areas of strength, you will be energized, more motivated about your work, and your self-esteem will be enhanced.

Create situations where you can spend a high percentage of time in your areas of strength. Then, give yourself regular feedback to reinforce the behaviors you want repeated. Doing this on a regular basis will produce an accumulative effect that will have a major impact on your performance, productivity, and results.

To focus on your strengths:

1. Have high expectations for yourself.
2. Find out what you do well and do more of it.
3. Find out what you do not do well and stop doing it.
4. Manage your weaknesses.

BUILD COMMITMENT

Developing personal leadership requires a dedication to your goals. Dedication to a task, goal, or a lifestyle starts with commitment. Winners say what they are going to do and do what they say. Losers make excuses. Vince Lombardi, the legendary football coach, said, "When the going gets tough, the tough get going." You need to pursue your dreams and goals with determination, dedication, and a certain toughness.

Robert Schuller wrote a book titled, *Tough Times Never Last, but Tough People Do*. You can overcome your tough times by having a purpose larger than yourself, by having written goals, and by sticking to your goals and plans with dogged determination, passion, persistence, and perseverance.

DO YOUR BEST

Doing your best is more about excellence than perfection. When you do your best and you know it, energy is generated that allows you to do even more in the future. When you accept less than the best from yourself and those you lead, you and your team members miss out on this energy rush.

HAVE FUN

Having fun isn't about frivolous activity; it's about having a passion and enthusiasm about your work in the same way you do about your hobbies or recreational pursuits. Be enthusiastic about and have a passion for your work, and it will be more fun. Instill the same kind of "having fun" mentality in your team members, and you'll have even more fun.

RECHARGE YOUR BATTERY

Perseverance is about finishing what you start. Ninety percent of all failure comes from not starting or quitting too soon. When you start something, perseverance is what causes you to persist. Thomas Edison said, "Many of life's failures are people who did not realize how close they were to success when they gave up." Brian Tracy said, "Sometimes your greatest asset is simply your ability to stay with it longer than anyone else."

It is difficult to persevere if you are tired. When your "battery" is run down or you are running on fumes, your mind is susceptible to negative thinking. In these circumstances, you are more likely to react, blow things out of proportion, and say things that you will regret.

Watch for the signs that you need to recharge your "battery," such as: tiredness, being easily frustrated, tension in your muscles, and feeling discouraged, to name just a few. Here are some things you can do to recharge your battery:

- Take a mental break: read or listen to inspirational or motivational material, spend some time on a hobby, call a friend, or listen to calming music.

- Take a physical break: rest, take a nap, go for a walk, eat something healthy, take some deep breaths, or exercise.

PUTTING PERSEVERANCE INTO ACTION

Put perseverance into action:

- When something bothers you, do not get frustrated.

- When you don't get the results you want, try again and again.

- Stay calm when something upsets you.

- Always finish what you start.
- Work a little harder or a few minutes longer on difficult tasks.

Are you fully committed to doing what you can to make a difference in your own life and achieve the goals that are important to you? The following poem speaks to the importance of perseverance in the face of obstacles and adversity:

DON'T QUIT

When things go wrong, as they sometimes will,
When the road you're trudging seems all uphill,
When the funds are low and the debts are high,
And you want to smile, but you have to sigh,
When care is pressing you down a bit-
Rest if you must, but don't you quit.
Life is weird with its twists and turns,
As every one of us sometimes learns,
And many a fellow turns about
When he might have won had he stuck it out.
Don't give up though the pace seems slow -
You may succeed with another blow.
Often the goal is nearer than
It seems to a faint and faltering man;
Often the struggler has given up
When he might have captured the victor's cup;
And he learned too late when the night came down,
How close he was to the golden crown.
Success is failure turned inside out -
The silver tint in the clouds of doubt,
And you never can tell how close you are,
It might be near when it seems afar;
So stick to the fight when you're hardest hit -
It's when things seem worst that you must not quit.

                                                    Unknown

KEEPING ON WITH PERSEVERANCE - SUMMARY

✓ Persistence, determination, and perseverance are all closely related and are key to developing personal leadership.

✓ Handle adversity by using your energy to remove or go around the obstacle rather than trying to place blame or be frozen in fear about the future.

✓ Focusing on your strengths will pay greater dividends than trying to "fix" your weaknesses.

✓ Enjoying a successful life requires a dedication to your goals.

✓ 90% of failure comes from not starting or quitting too soon.

KEEPING ON WITH PERSEVERANCE - AFFIRMATIONS

✓ I am determined to develop my personal leadership.

✓ I persevere toward the achievement of my goals.

✓ I focus on my strengths.

✓ I watch for signs that I need to recharge my battery.

✓ I start and finish things that are important to me.

Part III
Goal-Directed

Life is what we make of it. Consequently, if we want a successful life, it is up to each of us to create it. Success, however, doesn't just happen. Success is a result of both hard work and good planning.

Being goal-directed is a great way to create a successful life. Goals give us direction. They create purpose. Goals allow us to celebrate achievement and learn from our mistakes. Goals help us plan for our future, they maximize our success, and they stimulate top performance.

As you develop your personal leadership, ask yourself, "What are my goals?" "What am I working toward?" "What are my goals for tomorrow?" What are my goals in five years?"

Leaders have goals. They have something they are working toward. Their goals motivate them to do more and achieve more. With higher motivation, leaders are both driven and happy, which motivates those around them to set goals and become goal-directed.

In the next five chapters, you will learn how to become a goal-directed leader. You will explore the goals process, learn how to work smart, and uncover coaching techniques that will enable you to help others set and reach their goals, which will not only make them more successful, but empower you in the process.

9.
Clarifying Goals

*"Goal setting is the strongest human force
for self-motivation."*

- Paul J. Meyer

A farmer saw three young boys standing on the edge of a field of fresh snow. He offered a prize to the one who could walk the straightest line in the fresh snow.

The first boy thought if he watched each step, he would be able to walk a straight line. When he got to the other side of the field and looked back, he discovered that his steps had zigzagged and were not very straight.

The second boy learned from the first. He thought if he looked over his shoulder, he could see his tracks and keep his steps straight. He was disappointed to see his tracks were bowed as he made adjustments.

The third boy walked straight across the field and claimed his prize. When asked how he did it, he responded, "I saw a tree on the other side of the field and knew that if I looked at the tree, I could walk a straight line."

As you develop personal leadership, don't look at where you are now or where you have been. Instead, look at where you want to go.

THE BENEFITS OF SETTING GOALS

Having a written and specific goals program is one of the best ways to ensure your personal leadership. Once you start setting goals, you will begin to experience the many benefits that goal setting has to offer.

Goals create a sense of purpose

When you know where you stand, where you are going, and how you are going to get there, you have both a mission and a purpose. You have direction and feel in control. Without goals, you tend to wander and get caught in the "activity trap."

Goals save time

When your goals are clearly defined with specific action steps, you do not have to stop and think about what you are going to do next; it is clearly laid out for you.

Goals enhance and unleash creativity

Goals are not without obstacles, roadblocks, and hindering circumstances. When you look for ways over, under, or around your obstacles, you might discover new and better ways to do things. Many conveniences you enjoy today are the result of someone trying to solve a problem and, in the process, inventing a new product.

Goals provide direction

You will accomplish a lot more if you keep your eyes on a future goal, rather than spend time and energy thinking about where you are now or where you've been.

Goals help you set priorities

Base your priorities on your goals and action steps.

Goals draw resources to them

This is one of the most amazing benefits of setting goals. When you set a meaningful goal, your needs will be met. If you need people, you will find people. If you need money, you will find money. If you need ideas, you will generate ideas. If you need other resources, you will receive them. This could be called the "power of attraction." Set your goals, and they will come.

Goals reduce conflict

In *Atlas Shrugged*, Ayn Rand wrote, "There is no such thing as a contradiction (conflict). If you have what appears to be a contradiction, check your basic premises; one of them is wrong." When you have what appears to be a conflict, check your prioritized goals. Your most important goal will help you decide your best course of action.

Goals define winning

In sporting events, the team with the most points at the end of the game wins. In a successful life, when you achieve predetermined goals, you win. You do not necessarily have to beat someone else.

Goals maximize success and reduce failures

When you have a clearly defined target and a specific action plan to reach it, you are less likely to get off track or get derailed.

Goals pave the way to better decisions

The decisions you make will be based on your goals and where you stand in relation to their accomplishment.

GOAL SETTING PRINCIPLES

Goals need to be written

Writing crystallizes thought, and crystallized thought motivates action. When your goals are written, you can refer to them, communicate them, and create front-of-the-mind awareness.

Goals need to be specific

The mind can focus on something specific better than it can the abstract.

Goals need to be personal

You are more likely to take action on your own goals than you are on someone else's goals. When setting goals, make sure you tie your "ownership" to each goal.

I knew as early as junior high that I wanted to be a teacher and a coach when I grew up. Being active in sports, I knew that coaches helped bring out the best in people, encouraged others to set goals, and taught the importance of teamwork. I knew that my own skills as an athlete were greatly enhanced by the influence of the coaches in my life. I was a better player because of their coaching.

However, in the late '50s when I was in school, there was a great demand for engineers. Since I was good at math, there was a lot of pressure on me to pursue a career in engineering. Eventually, the pressure got to me, and I left a good teaching college and transferred to a good engineering school. Not only did I attend engineering classes, but I worked in the engineering department in the city of Akron, Ohio.

It wasn't until years later that I discovered that being an engineer was someone else's goal, not my own. Consequently, I left engineering and got into the people development business. With this move, a huge weight was lifted off my shoulders. I was happy. I was a teacher. A coach. I was pursuing MY goals and was successfully helping leaders bring out the best in themselves and those they lead.

Someone told me early in my career that if you don't have your own plan of action, you will end up with someone else's. This proved true for me, and I am glad I eventually decided to pursue my own goals.

Goals need to be positive
Set goals based on what you want to have happen instead of what you don't want to have happen.

Goals need to be measurable and contain a method for keeping score

Imagine that your goals are a sporting event. What will you put on the scoreboard during the contest or in the box scores the next day?

Goals need to be tangible and intangible

Tangible goals are goals to have. Intangible goals are goals to be or become. When possible, tie a tangible goal to each of your intangible goals and an intangible goal to each of your tangible goals. For example, if your tangible goal is to get a promotion, your intangible goal could be to develop more self-confidence.

You need to have long-range and short-range goals

Long-range goals give you direction and purpose. Short-range goals provide ongoing motivation, encourage action, and many times, are steps toward accomplishing long-range goals.

Goals need to have some stretch

If goals are too easy, they will not motivate you, and you may get bored. If goals are too difficult, they could cause stress and discouragement. For example, during a ring toss game, those who stood close and made almost every toss soon were bored and quit. Those who stood too far away and missed almost every toss soon were discouraged and quit. Those who stood at a challenging distance were the most motivated and played the longest. For optimum motivation, your goals need to have some stretch.

Goals need to contain action steps

Action steps become short-range or bite-sized goals and create motivation and momentum toward long-range goals. The completion of each action step can be cause for celebration.

Goals need to have a timetable, including deadlines

Deadlines increase focus, concentration, and stick-to-it-tiveness. Use them to your advantage.

WHY PEOPLE RESIST SETTING GOALS

There are many reasons why people resist setting goals. Some individuals don't know how to set goals. For others, it is a result of early childhood conditioning by parents, teachers, and other authority figures. In most cases, children do not set goals because their parents and teachers have always done it for them. Many times, bosses set goals for new employees. People are creatures of habit. If someone else sets goals for them until they are in their 20s, they get in the habit of not setting goals. Developing the habit of setting goals is not always easy, but it is necessary in order to develop your personal leadership.

Past mistakes and failures are another reason why individuals resist setting goals. If you have set unrealistic goals in the past, overestimated your ability to accomplish your goals, or underestimated what was required to accomplish them, you may resist setting new goals. The negative emotions that result from making a major mistake or experiencing a major set-back or failure are a strong conditioning factor to avoid such emotions in the future.

Some people have a need for predictability, which prevents them from setting goals. The loss of a "rut" can hold them back. The desire for a safe, secure environment and the fear of the unknown are strong factors to overcome. Many people like the comfort of the known and are overwhelmed by the fear of the unknown. If they do not set new goals, at least they know what to expect.

Other individuals are waiting for miracles and therefore don't set goals. "Wait" is a four letter word and can be a limiting factor when it comes to setting goals. I saw a quotation years ago that fits, "On the plains of hesitation lie the bleached bones of millions, who sat down to wait, and waiting, they died."

Since people do not like to be criticized or ridiculed, they think that if they do not set goals, no one can criticize them or ridicule them for not accomplishing them. This represents fear of losing. On the contrary, some people have trouble handling success and winning and therefore have a fear of winning. It comes from early conditioning and is real to them. The rationale is, "If I don't set new goals, I will not have to deal with these fears."

Finally, some people resist setting goals due to over-expectations. When you set goals so high that they are almost impossible to achieve in the timeframe established, you may rationalize by saying, "No one could have accomplished that goal, so I didn't even try."

TYPES OF GOALS

Personal	Family, financial, mental, physical, social, spiritual, and special
Business	Career & business development
Learning	What do you want to know?
Action-Oriented	What do you want to do? Where do you want to go?
Relationship	Develop new and/or improve existing; who would you like to meet?
Service	Who and where do you want to serve?
Continuous improvement	Personal development, systems, etc
Stretch	What do you want to do more of or better?

Having goals in every area of your life – career, family, financial, mental, physical, professional, social, and spiritual – will give you balance.

THE GOALS PROCESS

Now that you know what types of goals to set, let's take a look at the process for setting and achieving your goals. The following eight steps will provide some structure for setting and achieving goals:

1. Write your goal.
2. Set a target date for your goal.
3. List the benefits of accomplishing your goal.
4. List every possible obstacle.
5. Identify one or more solutions for each obstacle.
6. Write specific action steps with target dates.
7. Construct a method of keeping score or tracking your progress.
8. Write affirmations that support your goal.

KNOWING WHAT GOALS TO SET

If you are stumped on what personal goals to set, use the Dreams List and Goals Stimulator at the end of this chapter to get you started.

Observe what grabs and holds your attention. Clip pictures and articles of things that catch your eye in magazines and newspapers and put them in a file folder. After a period of time, lay out everything in the folder and see if you recognize a pattern.

Ask yourself the magic question, "If I had a magic wand and could have anything I wanted, what would I wish for?"

Keep a journal, notebook, or notepad handy. Write down possible goals as they occur to you. You can also carry a portable voice recorder to develop the habit of capturing goal possibilities. When you hear yourself say, "I wish…" or "I want to…" write down whatever comes next.

REDUCING PROBLEMS WITH WRITTEN GOALS

People do not perform at their best, if at all, in an environment of uncertainty. Uncertainty leads to stress, tension, and frustration. Frustration leads to anger. Anger leads to mistakes and damaged relationships. When these conditions exist, your energy is spent trying to reduce the tension instead of accomplishing the action steps that lead to the accomplishment of goals. When goals are written and specific, uncertainty is diminished, tension is reduced, and output flourishes.

When you set a goal and nothing gets in your way – there are no obstacles, set-backs, hindering circumstances, or roadblocks – you will accomplish your goal in the exact proportion to what you set out to accomplish. When your result is different than your goal, the difference can be defined as a problem.

Everyone has problems. A universal definition of a problem could be: the difference between a goal and a result. If people say they don't have problems, they are either kidding themselves or not exerting themselves. Problems go by many names: challenges, opportunities, crises, or troubles.

Definition of a Problem

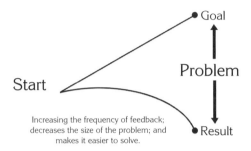

Increasing the frequency of feedback; decreases the size of the problem; and makes it easier to solve.

The sooner you recognize that you are not on track to reach your goal, the easier it is to take corrective action to repair the problem. People might say, "All of a sudden, I'm broke." They want you to believe that a giant vacuum cleaner emptied all of their accounts. This statement usually is not made when the problem is small; rather, it is made when the problem is so big that it overwhelms them. Translated, this means their outgoing expenses exceeded their income, and their upkeep became their downfall.

HOW TO MAKE GOALS MORE SPECIFIC

To make your goals more specific, use the Goals Ladder illustrated on the next page. Assume your goal falls somewhere between general and specific and put it in the middle of the ladder. Start by asking "why" questions to determine what is motivating you to accomplish your goal.

For example, a goal to get in better shape will mean different things to different people. If the reason why is to "look better," perhaps the real goal is plastic surgery or a better wardrobe. When the why is to "live longer," plastic surgery or a better wardrobe won't help.

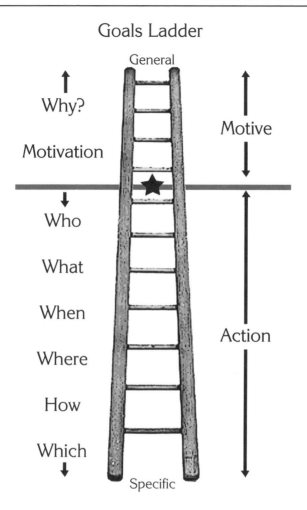

Goals Ladder

Once you know the why (reason, purpose, and motivation) for the goal, ask the who, what, when, where, how, and which questions. The "live longer" motive might require action steps to address diet, exercise, stress reduction, lifestyle changes, driving habits, regular medical exams, etc. The who might involve your cooking and eating habits. The what could include all areas. The when could be a schedule of events in priority order or in sequence. Ask enough questions to make sure the goal is specific enough. Not all goals will require asking all the questions. When it is right, you will know it.

PRIORITIES PREVENT PANIC

When goals and action steps are prioritized, there will be more "fire preventing" and less "fire fighting," more mid-course corrections and less "all of a sudden," and more celebrating and less panic. An effective technique for prioritizing goals is to write each goal on a separate 3x5 index card. Pick any two cards and determine which of the two is most important. Compare the one you chose to a third, and so on, until you have identified the most important one. Then, repeat the process to determine number two, three, etc., until you prioritize each step.

The time you invest in developing a written and specific goals program for yourself will pay big dividends in improved performance, productivity, and results.

Vince Lombardi, the legendary football coach, emphasized to his players, "You've got to get it in your head before you can get it in your feet." The same is true in business and interpersonal relationships. When you get it in your head – clearly, specifically, and succinctly positive actions will follow.

Results come from actions, and actions are determined by thoughts. When your thoughts are clear, you have a higher likelihood of getting the results you desire. At best, fuzzy thoughts produce fuzzy results. Usually fuzzy thoughts produce NO or POOR results. The clearer your goals, objectives, and expectations, the better your performance and results will be. The same is true for those you lead.

Priorities are important in one-on-one conversations, group presentations, training, writing goals, giving instructions, e-mails and reports, public relations, sales, customer

service, and most aspects of business and personal relationships. Our ability to prioritize has a definite impact on the
effectiveness of our communication.

Lee Iacocca, former Chairman of Chrysler Corporation, said, "You can have brilliant ideas, but if you can't get
those ideas across, they don't do anybody any good." To get
your ideas across, carefully choose your words, phrasing,
tone, and inflection. How a word or phrase is spoken can
dramatically impact your message and affect the thinking
(clear or fuzzy) of your audience.

Just as weeds choke out a garden and don't allow the
plants to grow, your productivity and effectiveness will be
diminished by "mental clutter" or fuzzy thinking. You can
stamp out "mental clutter" by:

1. Capturing your thoughts in writing

2. Having a written goals program with action steps

3. Distributing written expectations

4. Clarifying priorities for yourself and others

Fuzzy thoughts and "mental clutter" are conditions
that will drain your energy and contribute to worry, indecision, and procrastination. Clear thoughts will generate energy, stimulate action, and produce results. Clear thoughts
will also enhance communication, increase motivation, and
reduce mistakes and frustration.

HOW TO KEEP YOUR GOALS ALIVE

Set low goals and raise them gradually
This creates a sense of winning, which will boost self-confidence, self-image, self-esteem, and build enthusiasm for
new and larger goals.

Keep score
What is measured, tracked, and reported gets done. The way

you keep score can be as simple as hash marks, a barometer, a graph, or symbols, such as stars or smiley faces.

Schedule specific action steps
When you put things on your calendar in specific time slots, you are more likely to act on them. What gets scheduled gets done.

Set priorities
Tackle the most important action steps first.

Make public commitments
Let people who support you and your goals know what your goals are and what you are doing, or have done, to achieve them.

Ask for help if you need it
In the same vein that you miss 100 percent of the shots you do not take, you are not going to get much help with your goals unless you ask for it.

Use affirmations
An affirmation is a positive declaration stated as if it were true, regardless of whether it is actually true or false. Affirmations can help you achieve a goal because your subconscious mind cannot tell the difference between fact and fantasy. It believes anything it is told. It is also a servomechanism that guides your thoughts and behaviors. You can direct your subconscious mind to determine the behaviors necessary for the accomplishment of your goals.

Early in my sales career, I had large sales goals and used numerous affirmations to get mentally prepared for my future success. One of my affirmations was "I am a master salesman, a powerful closer, and people take action on my ideas." After a particularly trying day (zero for five), I stood in front of my mirror, repeated the above affirmation several times – and wanted to throw up! When you need an affirma-

tion the most is when it sounds the silliest.

Affirmations need to be written and read daily or memorized and recited daily. For best results, use the personal pronoun "I" and state your affirmations positively and in the present tense. Using the personal pronoun "I" addresses your subconscious mind. You may have been told not to overuse "I", but in this case, it is important to make certain your subconscious mind knows who you are talking to.

Stating your affirmations positively is important because your mind grasps positives better than negatives. For example, if you want to adjust your weight, it is better to say, "I weigh 160 pounds," rather than "I will lose 20 pounds."

Using the present tense takes advantage of the "act as if" principle. The subconscious mind responds well to positive, action-oriented commands. If you want to be happy, act happy. If you want to be enthusiastic, act enthusiastic. If you want to be energetic, act energetic. The "act as if" principle works when you use it.

CLARIFYING GOALS -
SUMMARY

✓ Having a written goals program is one of the best ways to develop your personal leadership.

✓ All good performance starts with clear goals, plus day-to-day monitoring.

✓ Writing crystallizes thought, and crystallized thoughts motivate action.

✓ You need to have short-range and long-range goals, as well as tangible and intangible goals.

✓ The use of affirmations is one of the best ways to support your goals program.

CLARIFYING YOUR GOALS - AFFIRMATIONS

✓ I have written and specific goals in every area of my life.

✓ I have short-range, long-range, tangible, and intangible goals.

✓ I have a system for monitoring the progress on my goals.

✓ I am passionate about achieving my goals.

✓ I use affirmations to support my goals.

DREAMS LIST

Write down everything you ever wanted to have, know, do, see, be, learn, places you want to go, things you want to achieve, recognition you want to receive, etc.

Do not give mental recognition to limitations. If something pops into your mind, write it down.

1.	26.
2.	27.
3.	28.
4.	29.
5.	30.
6.	31.
7.	32.
8.	33.
9.	34.
10.	35.
11.	36.
12.	37.
13.	38.
14.	39.
15.	40.
16.	41.
17.	42.
18.	43.
19.	44.
20.	45.
21.	46.
22.	47.
23.	48.
24.	49.
25.	50.

GOALS STIMULATOR

What do you want more of?
What do you want less of?
What do you want to improve?
Where do you want to go?
What do you want to do?
What do you want to learn?
Who would you like to meet?
What position would you like to hold?
What would you like to own?
What are your family goals?
What are your financial goals?
What are your mental goals?
What are your physical goals?
What are your social goals?
What are your spiritual goals?
What are your professional goals?
What are your personal development goals?
What are your earning goals?
What are your savings goals?
What are your investment goals?
What are your business goals?
Who would you like to help/serve?
What kind of lifestyle do you want?
What do you want to do for your parents?
What do you want to do for your children?
What do you want to do for your siblings?
What habits would you like to develop?
What would you like to do for recreation?
What kind of vacations would you like to take?
What kind of relationships do you want?
What skills would you like to develop?
What would you like to do for your community?
What is your passion?

10.
Planning Your Future

"By failing to prepare, you are preparing to fail."

- Benjamin Franklin

A daughter complained to her father about her life and how things were so hard for her. She did not know how she was going to make it and wanted to give up. She was tired of fighting and struggling. It seemed as one problem was solved, a new one arose.

Her father, a chef, took her to the kitchen. He filled three pots with water and placed each on a high fire. Soon the pots came to a boil. In one he placed carrots, in the second he placed eggs, and the last he placed ground coffee beans. He let them sit and boil, without saying a word.

The daughter sucked her teeth and impatiently waited, wondering what he was doing. In about twenty minutes, he turned off the burners. He fished the carrots out and placed them in a bowl. He pulled the eggs out and placed them a bowl. Then he ladled the coffee out and placed it in a bowl.

Turning to her, he asked, "Darling, what do you see."

"Carrots, eggs, and coffee," she replied.

He brought her closer and asked her to feel the carrots. She did and noted that they were soft. He then asked her to take an egg and break it. After pulling off the shell, she observed the hard-boiled egg. Finally, he asked her to sip the coffee. She smiled as she tasted its rich flavor.

She humbly asked, "What does it mean, Father?"

He explained that each of them had faced the same adversity, boiling water, but each reacted differently.

The carrot went in strong, hard, and unrelenting. But after being subjected to the boiling water, it softened and became weak.

The egg had been fragile. Its thin outer shell had protected its liquid interior. But after sitting through the boiling water, its inside became hardened.

The ground coffee beans were unique, however. After they were in the boiling water, they had changed the water.

"Which are you?" he asked his daughter. "When adversity knocks on your door, how do you respond? Are you a carrot, an egg, or a coffee bean? "

If you were planning a trip, you would want to know where you are now, where you want to go, and how you are going to get there. The same holds true when planning your future. To get started, you have to first determine where you stand now in every area of life: family, financial, mental, physical, social, and spiritual. Without a good understanding of where you stand currently and a vision of where you want to go, it will be difficult, if not impossible, to determine what your journey will be like.

A constant striving for more is what separates the highly successful from the average achievers. I assume since you are reading this book that you want to be more successful than you already are - you want to do more, be more, or have more. In order to do this, you must "plan your work and work your plan." Chances are, if you continue just as you are, you won't accomplish your goals.

If you want to have more or do more, you have to become more or better. To do this, start by visualizing your future. What does your ideal life look like a year from now, five years, ten years from now, or even longer?

According to author Malcolm Gladwell, achievement is talent plus preparation. Talent alone does not guarantee success. Success requires that you work smart, work hard, practice purposely, and that you overcome negative conditioning.

WORKING SMART

Working smart requires knowledge:

- **Knowledge about yourself** – your strengths, weaknesses, talents, desires, and goals.

- **Knowledge about people** – how to establish and maintain positive relationships.

- **Knowledge about your chosen work** – the benefits of your product or service, the skills necessary to excel at your job, and areas you need to improve.

- **Knowledge about your community, society in general, and current events** – be aware of your surroundings; you do not live in a bubble. People are influenced by their environment, and you will work smarter when you are aware of current events.

- **Knowledge about time management techniques** - such as being organized, planning ahead, working from priorities, staying in high payoff activities, and keeping the main thing the main thing.

Knowledge helps you read situations correctly and determine the best way to respond.

To work smart, surround yourself with people who encourage you, build you up, and support you in your pursuit of your goals. If possible, get a mentor or coach who can guide you. A good mentor or coach will put your best interest ahead of their own.

WORKING HARD

Working hard doesn't necessarily mean "back-breaking" labor or toiling for long hours. It means starting on time, being focused, sticking to your tasks, concentrating, eliminating distractions, and being in your zone.

PRACTICE PURPOSELY

Anyone who becomes great at anything – sports, music, business, parenting, selling, customer service, or any other job or task has had a goal to improve and has practiced purposefully. Practice doesn't necessarily make perfect, but it will lead to permanence. Sloppy practice will lead to sloppy habits. Purposeful practice will lead to improvement and, if practiced long enough, will lead to excellence.

In a study of people who had achieved greatness in many different fields, Daniel Levitin determined that 10,000 hours is the magic number necessary for greatness. Even if you're not striving for greatness, striving for mastery of your chosen field is a worthwhile goal. Like greatness, mastery also requires 10,000 hours of practice and execution.

Don't be overwhelmed by the 10,000 hours. If you practice purposefully and/or skillfully execute the skill you want to master eight hours a day, five days a week, you will master the skill in five years. How many hours will have elapsed in five years if you don't work on mastering your chosen skill? Exactly the same number of hours as if you had practiced purposely and skillfully executed the skill you wanted to master.

OVERCOMING NEGATIVE CONDITIONING

Negative conditioning from parents, teachers, friends, past mistakes, failures, and experiences can get in the way of preparing for achievement. To combat negative conditioning, make sure you have clearly defined, written goals that are important to you and a plan of action to achieve them. Guard your self-talk; make sure you reinforce the thinking that is necessary to achieve your most important goals. Remember, the way we think effects the way we act, and the way we act effects the results we get.

THE STEPS TO MASTERY

The key to mastery is the "next step." When you take enough steps in the direction of your dreams, you will achieve uncommon success because most people aren't willing to pay the price – in time and effort. In addition, focusing on the next step prevents you from feeling overwhelmed and keeps you focused on your goals.

Steps to Mastery

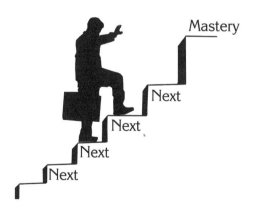

Jim Collins, author of *Good to Great*, points out that the biggest enemy of great is good. Debbie Fields, of Mrs. Fields Cookies fame, agrees with Jim Collins when she says, "Good enough never is." Former Michigan State football coach, Biggie Munn, posted a sign in the locker room that read, "The difference between good and great is a little extra effort."

When you think about a successful life and achievement, why be good when you can be great? Why would you want to be average when you can be awesome? Why be mediocre when you can be magnificent? Why be poor when you can be phenomenal? Why be ordinary when you can be extraordinary?

ENSURING FUTURE SUCCESS

Planning for your future will pay huge dividends as you develop personal leadership.

To help ensure future success:

- **Spend a lot of time in your primary areas of responsibility** - Resist the temptation to get distracted or drawn into low-payoff activities.

- **Focus on improving in the areas that you spend a lot of time** - If you are currently spending four hours per week in a given activity, improving your effectiveness by 10 percent will give you an extra 20 hours per year that can be invested in other high- payoff areas.

- **Invest as much time as possible in areas where you have the greatest strengths** - In addition to optimizing productivity, working in areas of your greatest strengths is more pleasurable and boosts your energy rather than drains it.

- **Stay in the moment** - Focus on where you are. The mind can only focus on one thing at a time. When you jump back and forth between multiple tasks or thoughts, you do not give either task or thought your full attention. When you do not give something your full attention, you will be less effective.

- **Use synergy** – When possible, combine several objectives into one activity.

- **Cut larger tasks into bite-sized chunks** - Large tasks can be daunting or overwhelming. When you break large tasks into bite-sized chunks you break inertia, overcome procrastination, and create momentum.

- **Start and finish strong** - Getting off to a fast start gives you momentum, motivation, and the confidence to continue. Finishing strong increases the likelihood of a successful conclusion.

- **Divide and conquer** - Isolate tasks that need your undivided attention. Set up separate folders, electronic files, or notebooks as needed.

- **Keep "could do" lists** - These are tasks or projects that you could do when you are blocked on your high-priority tasks or in downtime when you are away from your normal work area.

- **Organize and categorize** - Keep things you use on a regular basis in close proximity to your desk or work area. Set up and use a filing system that insures quick retrieval when you need them. Effective use of categories allows you to group similar tasks.

- **Simplify** - Look for ways to cut out steps, group similar activities, or otherwise streamline processes. Set up systems that will optimize flow and pave the way for accomplishment.

- **Manage distractions** - Clear the clutter, both physical and mental. Close your door. Change location. Turn off your computer monitor or close your laptop. Silence your phone.

  Additional techniques for managing distractions include: having written goals, setting deadlines and target dates, making and keeping commitments, and maintaining your energy level. '

PLANNING YOUR FUTURE - SUMMARY

✓ Having a plan for your future is an essential component for developing your personal leadership.

✓ Working smart requires knowledge.

✓ Purposeful practice will lead to improvement and, if practiced long enough, will lead to excellence.

✓ The way we think effects the way we act, and the way we act effects the results we get.

✓ The key to managing your time is managing yourself.

PLANNING YOUR FUTURE - AFFIRMATIONS

✓ I know where I stand, where I am going, and how I'm going to get there.

✓ I work smart.

✓ I work hard.

✓ I am taking the necessary next steps to master the skills necessary for developing my personal leadership.

✓ I am an organized "do it now" person.

11.
Stimulating Top Performance

"The best way to inspire people to superior performance is to convince them by everything you do and your everyday attitude that you are wholeheartedly supporting them."

- Harold Geneen

The whale trainers at Sea World are smarter than most managers. You may have observed that it is not natural behavior for a ten ton whale to leave the sanctuary of the water and jump twenty-two feet over a rope. But the trainers are very special people, and along with communicating to the whales that they care and have the whales' best interests at heart, they make a most important decision that we often overlook in business - they decide what they want the whales to do. It's very simple: jump over the rope. Then they begin to construct circumstances that will reinforce the behavior they seek to have repeated. They put the rope at a level where the whale can't possibly fail - on the bottom of the tank. When the whale swims over the rope, they feed it.

Over several months, they gradually move the rope upward, continuing to reward the whale for its successes, until it is making those spectacular leaps that audiences love to watch. How fast do they raise the rope? Slowly enough that the whale doesn't starve.

The result of this work is wonderful to behold - whales that leap twenty-two feet out of the water to the astonishment of the spectators and the gratification of the trainers. No doubt the whales enjoy it too.

ESTABLISHING APPROPRIATE LEVELS OF TRUST

Leadership is about personal relationships, and personal relationships are about trust. Trust is the feeling that we can depend on another person and is the single most important factor in personal relationships. To build appropriate levels of trust:

- Make and keep commitments. Say what you will do and do what you say.

- Meet deadlines. Give plenty of notice if you are going to miss a deadline.

- Be a good communicator.

- Eliminate fear of the unknown in your relationships.

- Be consistent.

- Avoid misunderstandings or fix them quickly if they do occur.

- Be fair.

- Steer clear of hidden agendas.

- Minimize confusion.

TEACHING TECHNIQUES THAT WORK

Too many workers are ineffective at doing their jobs. In most organizations, there are huge variations in performance. Quality initiatives take variations out of the manufacturing process and improve productivity. Effective leaders need to do the same thing with the performance of people.

Begin by looking for objective measures that are indicators of successful performance, such as revenue, production, waste, cost, safety, on-time deliveries, and customer and/or employee retention. Seek the answers to these questions: "What does this employee do?" "What is, or should be, his or her contribution to the organization?" "If no one, or someone else, was in this position, what would be different?"

Next, emphasize goal achievement. By focusing on goals and results, you can catch problems when they are small, help others make mid-course corrections, and provide training as needed.

Then, help people develop the skills necessary to be successful. Use the TSO formula for skills training:

Tell team members what needs to be done and why.

Show team members how to do the task, if necessary.

Observe team members performing the task. Once team members can do the job satisfactorily, return to focusing on goals and results.

Training Model

Tell  Show Observe

Finally, create an environment that offers opportunities for success. Remove obstacles, provide appropriate feedback, and be generous with your encouragement, praise, and recognition.

HELPING PEOPLE GET IN THEIR ZONE

People are in their ZONE when they appear to be working effortlessly and producing optimum results. When a job challenges an individual's abilities, the opportunity to be in the ZONE exists. When challenge is low and ability is high, individuals may become bored or distracted and may have a tendency to be sloppy and make mistakes. On the other hand, when a challenge is above an individual's ability level, it can cause stress, frustration, and tension, which leads to poor performance.

Getting Into Your Zone

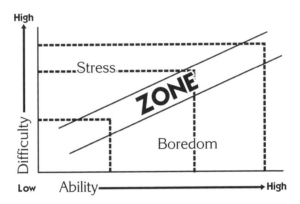

Individuals cannot be in their ZONE all the time. However, you can improve the probability of people being in their ZONE by appropriately matching jobs, challenges, and goals to skill levels.

When people are working in their ZONE, they are more productive, feel happier, use less energy, get better results, and are easier to coach. Here are some steps you can take to multiply the amount of time people are in their ZONE:

» Ask for an individual's absolute best in their areas of strength. People perform better when they work in their areas of strength because they feel more comfortable.

» Make sure others know what the goals are, what behaviors are necessary to achieve their goals, and what successful results look like.

» Point out and encourage progress.

Many people have personal problems that reduce their effectiveness on the job. In order to develop a high performing work force, it is critical that people feel good about themselves. Most people never receive the quality or quantity of recognition they deserve. Most people are not good at giving themselves a pat on the back, and it is easy for them to become discouraged.

Conversely, people who feel good about themselves are more productive and create more energy to achieve results in ways noticeable to you, their teammates, and most importantly, your customers.

PROCESS COACHING

When we hear the words coach or coaching, most of us think about sports. However, effective leaders use coaching techniques to improve performance and results. As you develop personal leadership, you will also create your own coaching style.

The following coaching process will help you as you develop personal leadership and create your own coaching style.

Coaching Process

Connect Concentrate Review Celebrate Help

CONNECT

Take time to connect with others. Start discussions with positive comments, observed improvement, and anything else that causes individuals to relax and creates an atmosphere of supportive rapport.

CONCENTRATE

Stay in the moment. Concentrate and resist the temptation to do or to think about anything besides what you can do to help the individual you are coaching at the moment.

REVIEW

Review results. What goals have been achieved? What actions steps have been completed? What encouragement can you offer?

CELEBRATE

Celebrate successes and improvements regularly.

HELP

Offer help and suggest new goals and action steps as needed. End the coaching session with ample encouragement and express your belief in the individual to get even greater results in the future.

CHARACTERISTICS OF EFFECTIVE COACHES

Very few coaches become great because they settle for being "good." Knowing how to support superior performance is critical to becoming a great coach. Assuming you have the right players on your team, the one characteristic on this list that will make most, if not all, of your goals a reality is bringing out the best in people. To do this, you must establish a level of mutual trust. Effective coaches:

- Bring out the best in people.

- Take players to levels they didn't think possible.

- Obtain commitments.

- Help others clarify and accomplish goals.

- Clarify thinking.

- Improve performance.
- Are committed to achieving results.
- Have the ability to make things happen.
- Know how to win.
- Celebrate successes and improvements.
- Focus on behaviors critical to individual and team performance.
- Have a desire to help people.
- Are available and willing to spend time with players.
- Have high expectations.
- Are credible, intelligent, and have a professional demeanor.
- Apply workable systems to every possible task.

THE SIX C's OF EFFECTIVE COACHING

Helping people grow, develop, and use more of their potential leads to improved performance and results. It also gives you and others numerous rewards – both tangible and intangible.

1. Confidence

People who have confidence in their ability, coach, organization, product and service, and industry outperform those who do not have confidence in these areas. Confidence gives them "bounce-back-ability" and allows them to overcome obstacles, hindering circumstances, or what other people say, think, or do. Those with less confidence are likely to avoid challenging situations and not perform to their fullest potential. A major responsibility of an effective coach is to help people develop more self-confidence. One of the most powerful tools for improving self-confidence is encouragement. Look for opportunities to encourage others.

2. Commitment

Great organizations and coaches have a firm commitment to improvement. Regardless of how good they are now, they want to be better. This commitment to improvement can be directed toward results and people. Are you committed to better results? Are you committed to helping your team members improve their performance and results? How do you express your commitment? Make firm commitments.

One of my favorite questions is, "Did you mean it when you said it?" Often, people will give lip service to their "commitments" or tell you what they think you want to hear. If you ask them, "Did you mean it when you said it?" when they say what they are going to do and/or when their behavior indicates they are not committed, it triggers them to re-think their commitment. Ask yourself the same question, "Did I mean it when I said it?"

3. Clarity

Clarity of thought is essential to extraordinary performance and results. Thoughts drive behaviors, and behaviors drive results. You can clarify your thinking by having discussions or brainstorming sessions with teammates and business associates. You can also commit your thoughts to writing. Keep a notepad, note cards, or a recorder with you to capture your thoughts. You never know when the solution to a problem or an idea for an opportunity will occur – so be prepared. Clarify your thinking.

4. Consistency

Consistency enables predictability, predictability enables trust, and trust enables performance improvement. Consistency gives most people comfort, and inconsistency causes them discomfort. If you say one thing and do another, people will feel unsettled. If you say or do something different under the same circumstance without explanation or good reason, people might question your sincerity. If you treat people differently under similar circumstances without explanation or good reason, people's "fairness streak" will surface, and their trust level toward you diminishes. Be consistent.

5. Continuous Improvement/ Change

It is jokingly said that people change in three ways: slowly, rarely, and never. It can also be said that people do not mind changing – they just do not like to be changed. Sidney J. Harris said, "Our dilemma is that we hate change and love it at the same time; what we want is for things to remain the same but get better." The reality is that there cannot be improvement unless something changes.

How to initiate change. People accept and support change more easily when they understand why change is necessary and when they are involved in the decision. It is important to inform employees of a decision early enough to make them feel important. Holiday Inn had a television ad years ago that promoted "the best surprise is no surprise." This is never truer than when you are implementing change.

How to accelerate change. People rarely want to change just because someone tells them to. Change is easier to accelerate when the individuals involved understand the need for change and how their performance impacts the desired change. It also helps when people understand the benefits and consequences of their performance. As a leader, it is your responsibility to make sure this understanding takes place.

Make sure you have the right people in place and that they are properly trained to handle their new responsibilities. Most individuals respond favorably when asked to implement change if they are properly trained to handle their new responsibilities.

How to make change stick. The culture of the organization is probably the most important element in making change stick. People are creatures of habit and continue to be driven by old habits until new ones are learned. Some things you can do to help develop the appropriate culture of change include:

- Reinforcing positive behavior and improvements

- Building on successes

- Removing threats

- Keeping communication lines open

- Having a written plan of action, including expectations

- Encouraging a team environment of "we" rather than "I' or "they"

- Having a compelling vision, mission, and purpose

Accept, embrace, and encourage change.

6. Confronting

Many people think confrontation is negative. They recall childhood sayings, such as: "If you cannot say anything nice about someone, don't say anything at all" or "Play nice." These thoughts can get in the way of appropriate confrontation.

If people's behavior is inappropriate, you do them a disservice by not bringing it to their attention. Most, if not all, people want to know if their behavior is counter-productive for achieving the desired results and contributing to the team's success. Here are some guidelines for effective confrontation:

- Focus on specific issues or behaviors the individual can control. Avoid personal attacks.

- Deal with the facts. Avoid using rumors, innuendos, or sarcasm as a basis for confrontation.

- Avoid inflammatory words such as should, ought to, have to, always, or never.

- Train yourself to listen for what is important or key to the issue, and "block" inflammatory words.

- Be direct without being rude, obnoxious, or otherwise offensive.

- Treat the individual with dignity and respect; resist showing your anger. Keep in mind, people will always remember how you made them feel long after the words are forgotten.

- Help the individual develop a plan of action for correcting an unproductive situation and get a commitment from the individual to do so.

- Approach the situation as soon as you have the facts and the opportunity to meet privately with the individual.

- End your coaching session by stating your belief that the individual will do better in the future.

Care enough to confront.

OPENING CLOSED MINDS

Sometimes during training, confronting, and other aspects of coaching, people become stubborn, defensive, and hard to communicate with. They convince themselves that they are right, and as a result, have a closed mind. To open closed minds, find an area that you both agree on. Agreement tends to open minds, while opposition or adversity tends to close minds.

You can also find an area where you can let the individual be right. One of the strongest desires of most people is to be right. Try to understand what is important to people and help them be right. Always avoid the closed-minded position of saying, "I'm right." Instead, say, "You might be right." Then, listen to what they have to say. Perhaps with clarification you will come to understand their position, or they will recognize that there might be another side to the issue. Instead of telling someone they are wrong, which tends to produce defensiveness, say, "I see it differently."

Avoid using logic on a closed mind. Logic has a tendency to produce point/counterpoint type arguments when you are dealing with a closed mind.

When presenting evidence, select the appropriate time. Usually, the best time is when the individual has started to open his/her mind.

The real difference in effective coaching is not education, knowledge, power, or talent. Effective coaching includes believing in others, taking a genuine interest in them and their success, listening to them, encouraging them, and making them feel special. It is about doing whatever it takes to help them be their best and boost productivity.

Effective coaching can reduce or eliminate problems. For coaching to be effective, be sure to clarify your expectations in writing and remember to keep it simple. Focus on goals and results and both give and ask for feedback. In regard to deadlines and target dates, it is important to inspect what you expect. Provide the individual with a preliminary target date if review and feedback are required.

Positive feedback is essential for growth and should be plentiful. When providing positive feedback, be sure to include feedback for outstanding performance, improved performance, and continuing performance. All three are signs of improvement.

To stop undesirable behaviors, use negative injunctions. Confronting the individual shows that you care. Do not wait. Confront the individual as soon as possible and identify the wrong action. Confront only what the person can change and be sure to give the person the benefit of the doubt. When providing feedback, be specific, avoid sarcasm, and eliminate words such as always and never. Tell the person how you feel about what was done wrong. Then working together, develop a game plan to fix the problem. End the session by affirming him or her as a person.

LEADERSHIP PRINCIPLES

Do you have what it takes to be a good leader? Can you take people from where they are to where they want to be? Can you help people improve their performance and results?

The following principles will help you stimulate top performance in both yourself and others:

Clarify your goals.
Know what you want to accomplish and what good performance looks like.

Help others clarify their goals.
Make sure they know how they will benefit by improving their performance.

Paint the big picture.
Use word pictures, examples, stories, and analogies to help people visualize what good performance looks like. Vince Lombardi told his players, "You've got to get it in your head before you get it in your feet."

Help others clarify their thinking.
Be as specific as possible with your instructions. State them in terms of desired outcomes.

Encourage commitments.

Get people to face up to what they say they want. Use short-range, next step targets like today, tomorrow, and this week. Short-term commitments intensify motivation and create a sense of urgency.

Create a motivating environment.

Guide people to focus on what they want to accomplish and why they want to accomplish it.

Be generous with your encouragement.

People will achieve in direct proportion to their self-image and self-esteem. By pointing out progress, giving positive feedback, and challenging them to reach greater heights, you can encourage them to put forth extra effort. A self-image, once stretched, will not return to its former shape. The elixir for expanding a person's self-image is encouragement.

Identify and help remove obstacles to growth.

Help people determine their high-payoff activities and then guide them to spend more time working in these areas.

Sell or be sold.

You will probably hear many "namby-pamby" excuses on why people do not perform well. To offset this tendency, adopt the motto, "Action, not promises. Results, not excuses."

Have confidence in your information.

People need to believe that you know what you are talking about. Your confidence level provides them with the incentive to do what needs to be done.

Almost all individuals in a leadership role can substantially improve their leadership techniques and thus, their results. It is mainly a matter of conscious choice and a willingness to examine what personal behaviors need to change.

STIMULATING TOP PERFORMANCE - SUMMARY

✓ Establishing trust is essential for stimulating top performance.

✓ You can help people develop the skills necessary to be successful by teaching, showing, and observing.

✓ To stimulate top performance, you need to support and recognize superior performance.

✓ You can open closed minds by letting the other person be right.

✓ Being generous with encouragement is a great way to stimulate top performance.

STIMULATING TOP PERFORMANCE - AFFIRMATIONS

✓ I strive to build trust with others.

✓ I emphasize goal achievement.

✓ I create an environment that offers opportunities for success.

✓ I effectively confront inappropriate behavior.

✓ I try to always bring out the best in myself and others.

12.
Maximizing Your Success

"When you have the courage to keep score, you are guaranteed to win more."

A manufacturing company had a horrendous absenteeism problem. It was costing them a lot of money in overtime and temporary services. Mistakes were being made, and they were losing customers. Management tried everything they could think of to correct the problem but were without success. During a management development process, the problem surfaced, and the facilitator asked some insightful questions that produced startling results.

His questions involved who, what, when, where, how, and why. When he got to "When is it occurring?" the answer was "We don't know.", and he said, "Let's find out."

The team gathered statistics from the previous six months and presented them several different ways. When they looked at the per day statistics, the insight paid off. They found that Monday through Thursday attendance was in an acceptable range, but Friday attendance missed the mark drastically.

When the managers were asked why they thought this was happening, they said it was probably because they paid people on Thursdays. When asked why they did that, the classic response was because we've always done it that way. When asked what would happen if they changed payday to Fridays, the response was "We don't know." The facilitator said, "Let's find out." They changed payday to Fridays, and their absenteeism problem shrunk to an acceptable size. The benefits were substantial. Without the insight, the problem would probably still exist today, or worse yet, they would be out of business.

DEFINING WINNING ON YOUR TEAM

In sports, winning usually involves outperforming other teams or individuals. The same could be said for business – for example, winning is outperforming your competition. However, winning in business does not have to be limited to beating the competition. Perhaps winning is achieving certain pre-determined goals such as sales, profit, customer satisfaction, customer or employee retention, quality products, innovations, new products or services, and market penetration.

What is the "Super Bowl," a world championship, or points leader in your business? Can you state it in specific terms? Do all the members of your team know the goals and how to articulate them? Are all members on your team keeping score on results and activities that contribute to team success? Is their scorekeeping aligned with and supportive of yours?

What behaviors do you need team members to start to achieve greater results? What behaviors do you need team members to stop? What behaviors are team members doing well that you want them to do more of? What scorecards can you put into place that will ensure more of the behaviors you want?

WHAT WE CAN LEARN FROM THE WORLD OF SPORTS

Have you noticed that scoreboards keep getting bigger and bigger and that they contain more information? Sportscasters on radio and television broadcast all kinds of performance and results information, including win/loss records and individual and team statistics. Players and teams keep their own information on all aspects of their performance. Why? So they can improve their performance and results. When they improve performance and results, they provide more value and make more money.

You can improve performance and results in your business by improving your scorekeeping system. You must define what winning is in your business, identify the key function indicators or critical success factors that lead to winning, and establish a scorekeeping system that is simple, visual, objective, and current.

THE ROLE OF STATS

Unfortunately, in business, too many people think they are too busy "working" to keep statistics. When you keep track of the appropriate statistics and monitor them on a frequent basis, you can work smarter instead of harder, and you will have more time for important tasks.

Championship athletes and teams keep statistics to improve performance and results. In basketball, statistics include shooting percentage (field goals, 3 point, and free throws), rebounds, steals, assists, and turnovers. In baseball, it is batting averages, earned runs averages, slugging percentage, on-base percentage, stolen bases, walks, strikeouts, and fielding average. Similar categories exist in every sport.

Ask yourself, do you have lingering problems that you have not been able to solve or goals you have been unable to reach? Take a new look at statistics that are available to you and/or set up a scorekeeping system to get new statistics. Electronic spreadsheets are a great way to look at a set of statistics in many different ways so you can gain additional insight.

BENEFITS OF KEEPING SCORE

Scorekeeping is so popular because it offers so many benefits for everyone involved.

Keeping score generates excitement for players and fans
Scorekeeping improves individual and team performance, enhances concentration and focus, helps coaches and players make better decisions, helps prevent and solve problems, identifies opportunities for training, and makes it easier to accurately project outcomes.

Keeping score provides early warning signals
The gauges on the dashboard of your vehicle provide a form of keeping score. They indicate how much fuel you have, how well your engine is performing, and whether it needs maintenance. The odometer indicates how far you have driven – overall and on a given trip. A thermostat is used to keep score on the room temperature and adjusts the heat or air conditioning accordingly. In business, it is crucial to have a method of keeping score in place that provides early warning signals so you can make the appropriate adjustments.

Keeping score helps break goals into bite-sized chunks
This promotes confidence when people think and say, "I can do that." Knowing that you are winning at small goals helps build momentum and increase your opportunities to accomplish larger goals.

Keeping score provides trends and direction
Where you are now is important. Even more important is what direction you are moving and at what speed. Knowing trends and direction helps reduce the chance of surprises and uncertainty. Increased certainty enhances confidence, and increased confidence promotes increased success.

Keeping score helps you celebrate successes
One response to seeing the score is "Hooray!" When you

reinforce "Hooray," progress and success are reinforced. Reinforcing progress and success creates a motivational environment that leads to more progress and success.

Keeping score can help you take corrective action
Another response to seeing the score is "Oh no." Following "Oh no" situations with a corrective plan of action including additional training and coaching reduces future "Oh no's."

Keeping score enhances change
Keeping score creates insight, and insight precedes change. When you know where you stand and what direction you are heading, you can set new goals, adjust your behavior, and produce new or better results.

Keeping score improves accountability
When a good scorekeeping system is in place, people can run, but they can't hide.

KNOWING WHAT TO KEEP SCORE ON

Once you have made the decision to start keeping score, you need to determine what to keep score on. To get started, ask yourself a series of questions that include:

» What are the most important measures of success in our business?

» What areas directly or indirectly impact productivity?

» What areas directly or indirectly impact profitability?

» What defines winning for our team?

» What factors contribute to our winning?

» What do we want more of?

» What do we want less of?

» What levels of performance need to improve?

You can also determine areas on which to keep score by examining problems:

» When does the problem occur?

» Where does the problem occur?

» What is causing the problem?

» Why is the problem occurring?

METHODS FOR KEEPING SCORE

There are several different methods that can be utilized for keeping score. It is up to you to determine which method will work best for you.

Graphs
Line graphs are best for showing trends and direction as well as deviation from a norm, standard, or goal. Bar graphs are good for showing comparisons to previous periods. Pie charts are good for comparing the relationship of items to the total.

Hash marks
Sometimes scorekeeping can be as simple as putting hash marks or other symbols on a calendar. For example, you could keep track of the number of orders per day or put a symbol on every day that is over a certain number. The same could be done for dollar volume, units produced, and many other factors.

Barometers
A barometer can show progress toward a goal for a predetermined period such as weekly, monthly, quarterly, or annually. As you generate revenue, complete procedures, produce units, or do whatever you are tracking, you can color the appropriate increment on the barometer, similar to fund-raising

billboards.

SCOREKEEPING PRINCIPLES

The main purpose of keeping score is to improve performance and results. Make sure you use your scorekeeping system to solve problems, not to find fault. Once problems are identified and defined, use the insight you gain from keeping score to decide what corrective actions are needed.

The following principles are essential when keeping score:

Keep it simple

If keeping score requires too much time or too many complicated calculations, people may be reluctant to keep score. Remember the KISS principle – Keep It Short and Simple.

Keep it visual

A common thought is that a picture is worth a thousand words. Likewise, a graph can be worth a thousand words or numerous columns of numbers. Visual scorekeeping means displaying the score prominently as well as graphically.

Keep it objective

In most sporting events, the score is rarely, if ever, in dispute. The same kind of certainty and objectivity is needed in business scorekeeping. A subjective goal such as improved communication or morale can be quantified by answering the questions, "What will be different when communication is improved?" or "…when morale is improved?" For example, there might be fewer mistakes, enhanced quality, better attendance, or improved employee retention.

You can also use the electronic scoreboard concept. If you had an electronic scoreboard at the end of your work area, similar to a football scoreboard, what would you put on it to know that you are winning?

Keep it current

Most things in life are better when they are new and fresh. The same is true with scorekeeping in business. Week old, or even day old, numbers are not as good as "freshly baked," same day numbers or statistics.

USING RESOURCES EFFECTIVELY

You have certain resources available to you to do your job. These may include time, people, money, equipment, products, and facilities. The better you use your resources, the more productive you will be. Make sure that effective use of resources is a major part of your scorekeeping system.

For example, the results a football coach wants for his running backs is yards gained; the main resource a running back has to gain yards is "carries." When the number of yards gained is divided by the total number of carries, the running back's scorecard would be "yards per carry." To ensure quality as well as quantity, a second scorecard could be, "number of successful carries between fumbles."

When you know the results you want each person on your team to accomplish and you know the most valuable resources available to each person, you can help them set up meaningful scorecards.

GETTING FEEDBACK ON YOUR PERFORMANCE

Scorekeeping can be a great tool to improve individual performance, as well as team performance. You do not have to wait on feedback from your coach; you can give yourself feedback based on your scorecards.

Determine what results you want your team to accomplish. Identify the most valuable or expensive resources your team has available to them that will produce these results and develop scorecards that will give you feedback on the results you are getting and/or the progress you are making toward the results.

Ken Blanchard and Spencer Johnson, in *The One Minute Manager*, wrote that feedback is the "breakfast of champions." Championship performance requires feedback, and keeping score on your success factors is a great source of feedback.

MAXIMIZING YOUR SUCCESS - SUMMARY

✓ You can improve performance and results in your business by improving your scorekeeping system.

✓ In business, it is crucial to have a method of keeping score in place that provides early warning signals so you can make the appropriate adjustments.

✓ Make sure you use your scorekeeping system to solve problems, not to find fault.

✓ The better you use your resources, the more productive you will be.

✓ You can give yourself feedback based on your scorecards.

MAXIMIZING YOUR SUCCESS - AFFIRMATIONS

✓ I work smarter instead of harder by keeping score.

✓ I define winning.

✓ I utilize the resources available to me.

✓ I develop scorecards.

✓ I track my progress.

13.
Keeping the Main Thing the Main Thing

"If you want to make good use of your time, you've got to know what's most important and then give it all you've got."

- Lee Iacocca

I tried to climb the mountain today. As I inched my way up the path, I felt overwhelmed, so I had to turn back.

I tried to climb the mountain today. On my journey, darkness started to fall, and I was full of fear, so I had to return to a safe place.

I was ready to climb the mountain today. But it was so hot outside, I thought I better stay in my nice air-conditioned house and rest up for tomorrow's attempt.

I was about to climb the mountain today. But I had so many other things to do, so instead of climbing the mountain I took care of much more important tasks. I washed my car, mowed the grass, and watched the big game. Today the mountain will just have to wait.

I was going to climb the mountain today. But as I stared at the mountain in its majestic beauty, I knew I stood no chance of making it to the top, so I figured why even bother trying.

I had forgotten about climbing the mountain today, until a friend came by and asked me what I was up to lately. I told him I was thinking about climbing that mountain some day. I went on and on about how I was going to accomplish this task.

Finally, he said, "I just got back from climbing the mountain. For the longest time, I told myself I was trying to climb the mountain but never made any progress. I almost let the dream of making it to the top die. I came up with every excuse of why I could not make it up the mountain, but never once did I give myself a reason why I could. One day as I stared at the mountain and pondered, I realized that if I didn't make an attempt at this dream, all my dreams will eventually die."

"The next morning, I started my climb." He continued, "It was not easy, and at times I wanted to quit. But no matter what I faced, I placed one foot in front of the other, keeping a steady pace. When the wind tried to blow me over the edge, I kept walking. When the voices inside my head screamed "stop!" I focused on my goal, never letting it out of sight, and I kept moving forward. At times, I was ready to quit, but I knew I had come too far. Time and time again, I reassured myself that I was going to finish this journey. I struggled to make it to the top, but I climbed the mountain!"

"I have to be going," my friend said. "Tomorrow is a new day to accomplish more dreams. By the way, what are you going to do tomorrow?"

I looked at him, with intensity and confidence in my eyes, and said, "I have a mountain to climb."

THE CONCEPT OF TIME

Time is a true equalizer. All people have 24 hour days – no more and no less. How you use that time determines your accomplishments, productivity, happiness, and success.

It is a misnomer to think that you can manage time. You can manage yourself with self-discipline. You cannot really manage other people. You can manage your agreements with them. You cannot effectively manage your environment or circumstances. You can manage your attitude and your responses to circumstances and the environment.

You have more control over how you spend or invest your time than you might think. You control most of your free time, how much energy you exert, your attitude, your thoughts and imagination, what you say, how you say it, how you look, how you act, who you choose as role models, who you spend your leisure time with, your commitments, the causes to which you give your time, your concerns and worries, your response to difficult times and people, and your relationships. Instead of trying to manage your time, focus on doing a better job of managing yourself.

YOU CAN DO ANYTHING YOU WANT – BUT NOT EVERYTHING

Most people have the ability to do a lot of different things. When you have clearly defined goals, good coaching, and you practice, practice, practice, you can excel at almost anything you choose. However, when you try to excel in too many things, something suffers.

When a heart beats excessively faster than normal, the blood is blocked rather than pumped through it. This condition is called fibrillation. By rushing through tasks, activities, meetings, and days, for example, you might be defeating your larger purpose and not accomplishing your greater goals.

Excessive and continuous rushing can cause heart disease, high blood pressure, and other ailments, which will actually take more time in the long run. To offset the tendency to rush excessively, try the following:

- Plan some buffer time in your schedule.

- Develop a hobby or recreational pursuit.

- Reward yourself for creating balance in your work schedule and life.

- Schedule quiet time where you can listen to your body, your feelings, and your intuition.

There is something to say about the old saying "Steady wins the race." It is possible to lead such a frantic life that you don't accomplish nearly what you are capable of. You are bombarded with messages to hurry up, try harder, time is running out, get more done in less time with less people, and many more. When speed is the single focus, mistakes are made, you don't do your best work, quality suffers, relationships suffer, and a feeling of helplessness sets in.

In addition, when you put too much emphasis on one area of your life to the detriment of other areas, the imbalance can cause an energy drain, a strain on relationships, health issues, and ultimately, even damage to your emphasis area. To ensure your success, it is essential to create balance in your life and minimize the amount of time you spend rushing through tasks and activities.

COMMON TIMEWASTERS

Since we are unable to add more time to our days, it is advantageous that we decrease or eliminate things that waste our valuable time, such as:

- Attempting too much

- Procrastination; delaying distasteful tasks

- Indecision

- Unclear communication

- Perfectionism; too much attention to detail
- Preoccupation with problems
- Not actively listening
- Excessive socializing
- Lack of, or ineffective, delegation
- Constant checking on employees
- Inability to say "no"
- Unnecessary or unproductive meetings
- Allowing constant interruptions by others
- Insisting on knowing all and seeing all
- Assistant not aware of changes in schedule
- Allowing upward delegation
- Doing other people's work
- Not effectively training staff
- Firefighting (80% of "crisis management" events are preventable)
- Insufficient planning, scheduling, or organizing
- Relying on mental notes
- Not effectively utilizing waiting time and travel time
- Inefficient office layout
- Facts, phone numbers, and other vital information not at hand
- No daily plan
- No self-imposed deadlines
- No follow-up system
- Lack of procedures

- Not using prime time for priority items
- Spending time on low-priority items
- Lack of written goals or poorly defined goals
- Not enough "quiet time"

USING TIME EFFECTIVELY

Thinking, Planning, and Organizing

Thinking, planning, and organizing helps you do things when, or before, they need to be done. Schedule time for thinking, planning, and organizing on a daily basis.

Written Goals and Action Steps

Having written goals and action steps gives you a sense of direction, causes you to stretch, and provides the motivation to perform better.

Reduce Mental Clutter

The mind can only crystallize one thought at a time. When you are multi-tasking, your mind is jumping back and forth between the multiple activities, causing static and clutter in your mind. When this happens, some mental power is lost. Focus on one priority item at a time. Remove physical clutter or distractions. Focus and concentrate by taking notes or asking questions.

Be Flexible

Allow time for interruptions, distractions, and unexpected emergencies. Build in buffer time for projects, meetings, larger tasks, and travel. When you do not need the buffer time, you will have bonus time to complete other priorities.

Know and Use Your Most Productive Times

Keep a time log or time picture for five to ten days. Observe when you seem to be the most productive and start scheduling important activities accordingly.

Use Deadlines

Is it not amazing how much you can get done the day before you are leaving on vacation? That is the power of deadlines and impending events. Use deadlines to spur your energy and productivity. Set time limits for projects and tasks. Use natural dividers such as within the hour, by noon, by the end of the day, before you take a break, and any other criteria that will create a sense of urgency.

Break Larger Tasks into Bite-sized Chunks

The old saying "you eat an elephant one bite at a time" is true when it comes to using your time effectively. Alan Lakein called it the "Swiss cheese" method where you work on the pieces in odd moments that would otherwise be unproductive.

Learn to Say "No"

Saying "yes" when you would rather say "no" causes stress. Saying "no" doesn't mean you do not like the person, just that you are refusing their current request. Focus on your goals and priorities and avoid these distractions. When you give a loud and clear "yes" to your goals and priorities, it will be easier to say "no" to less important activities.

» Just say "no." Be direct and succinct. Simply say "no thank you."

» Give a brief and genuine reason for your no.

» If you are willing to say yes at a later date, offer a rain check.

Reward Yourself

Reinforcing the behaviors you want repeated is a tried-and-true technique. If your environment does not provide this kind of feedback, do it yourself.

Manage Stress and Boredom

You do not perform at your best when you are experiencing

stress or boredom. Stress usually comes from taking on too many things at once or trying to perform in areas too difficult for your current level of ability or current resources. Boredom usually comes from being involved in mindless activities that do not challenge your ability or resources. To stay in your "ZONE," match the difficulty level of your activities with your ability level and resources.

The Organizer Misnomer
Software or handhelds do not organize, people do. Software and handhelds are just places to store what you have organized. Technology can speed up sorting, scheduling, and other functions, but only you can organize your thought processes and priorities.

Avoid "Rushing"
Pace yourself. Remember, "Steady wins the race."

Make and Keep Commitments
In addition to making you feel good about yourself, making and keeping commitments will build trust and improve your relationships.

Practice "Fire Prevention" Instead of "Fire Fighting"
In many organizations, "fire fighting" is unwittingly encouraged and reinforced. People are recognized and rewarded for solving problems that should not have happened in the first place while people who prevent "fires" go unnoticed and unrecognized. Prior planning prevents poor performance. By planning for contingencies and what might go wrong, many problems can be prevented. Look for ways to recognize and reward those who plan and prevent problems.

Do a Time-Study Analysis
A time-study analysis will allow you to see where you are spending your time. To conduct the analysis, write down what you are doing every day. Be as candid and accurate as possible. Use the smallest increments possible and note

all occurrences. A minimum of five days is recommended. Repeating this periodically will help you fine-tune how you invest your time.

Practice Job Improvement Daily
If you invest five minutes per day and five days per week to make one improvement in your job, you will have 1,200 improvements over a five-year period.

Play "Ask Your Supervisor"
Have the courage to ask your boss, "How do you know when I'm doing a good job?" and then ask the follow-up question, "What can I do to improve?"

Master E-mail
Use this fantastic tool, but don't let it control you. It is estimated the average business person receives 80 e-mails a day, and many feel that 80 percent of the messages are of little or no value. Ask to be removed from various lists, including unnecessary "cc" lists and unwanted solicitations. Consider getting a separate e-mail address for important messages. Avoid checking e-mails as they arrive. Check your e-mail once or twice a day or on a schedule that works for you.

Deal with e-mail immediately upon opening it if possible. If it requires a quick response, reply and delete or file. When appropriate, forward the message to someone else to handle. If a message requires some time to respond, save it or print it and schedule time to handle it in your planner.

TIME SAVERS

When used properly, the following activities can save time and allow you to spend more time on more important tasks.

Planning
One hour of planning will save 10 hours of doing. Writing

crystallizes thought, and crystallized thought motivates action. Writing bridges the conscious and the subconscious mind.

Speed Reading

The average reading speed is approximately 200 words per minute. The average person reads two hours per day. Improving your reading speed from 200 words per minute to 400 words per minute will save an hour a day. Assuming a 240-day work year, this is the equivalent of 30 eight-hour work days. What could you accomplish with an extra 30 work days per year? Considering these findings, please do not say you do not have time to take a speed reading course.

Meetings

Effective meetings can be invigorating, stimulating, productive, and vital to the success of your organization. Ineffective meetings can be de-motivational, energy draining, morale killing, frustrating, and huge time wasters. Here are some things you can do to make sure your meetings are productive:

- Make sure only those needed in the meeting are invited.

- Always use a written agenda and distribute it in advance of the meeting. Use it to keep the meeting on schedule and to take notes of actions needed, commitments made, and results achieved.

- Set and stick to specific starting and ending times.

If you are participating in a meeting where you are not in charge and you feel you have made all the contributions you can make, ask if there are any further contributions you can make. If not, excuse yourself and leave.

THE POWER OF FOCUS AND CONCENTRATION

Just as a pair of binoculars, a telescope, or a magnifying glass helps you see things better, focus and concentration help you be more productive. The mind can only crystallize one thought at a time. When you jump back and forth between tasks or thoughts, you use energy that could otherwise be used to accomplish the most important task. Your thinking becomes diffused or hazy, and hazy thoughts get hazy results, at best, and typically produce no results. Crystallized thoughts stimulate creativity, generate energy, and produce the desired results.

When you are concentrating, you are using your mind's eye to bring clarity to your ideas, find answers to your questions, and find solutions to your problems.

Most highway accidents are caused by someone's lapse in concentration. Most quality and safety issues are also caused by someone's lapse in concentration.

Concentration is the key to power in physics. Likewise, concentration is the key to improving performance and results in every area of your life. When you consistently concentrate on the areas of your work that have the greatest potential instead of paying equal attention to everything and everybody, you will be much more productive. Stay in the moment when you are working on tasks. Stay in the moment during individual and group meetings. Stay in the moment when you are on phone calls. The time it takes to stay in the moment will save you time in the long run. Wherever you are, be there.

STAY IN THE MOMENT

Focus and concentration are critical to success in most undertakings, and it is especially critical in human relationships. When you "multi-task," i.e. think about something else, check your e-mail, read a report, or do anything else while you are conversing with someone in person or by phone, you are not focusing or concentrating. Two things can happen, and neither is good:

- The other person will sense it and could feel devalued and/or

- You might miss something crucial to the relationship or issue being discussed.

Either of these outcomes can hamper productivity, lower the quality of work, and damage an important relationship. Listed below are 16 tips for staying in the moment. Pick one or more that might be an issue for you and make a concentrated effort to improve. Then, pick another and continue the process until you are a master at staying in the moment.

1. Focus on what the other person is saying. Pay attention to tone, inflection, phrasing, speed, volume, etc. Try to match the other person without being obvious.

2. Use the other person's name.

3. Paraphrase

4. Make eye contact.

5. Face the other person squarely; avoid turning your shoulders as if you're trying to leave, looking at your watch, etc.

6. Eliminate distractions.

7. Ask questions; pause and let the other person answer.

8. Talk less; don't interrupt.

9. Avoid being judgmental or thinking about what you'll say next; if you pause after someone speaks or asks a question, it will appear that you are giving the person's thought or question careful consideration and, at the

same time, it will give you time to think of a response.

10. Acknowledge key points with nods and/or phrases ("I see," "I understand," "Right," "Makes sense," etc.).

11. Resist jumping to conclusions or pre-judging.

12. Ask relevant, open-end questions, e.g. "What do you mean by that?" "When you say...?" or use statements like "Tell me more," and "Tell me about it."

13. Act like the other person is the most important person in the world; at this moment, he or she is.

14. Set a goal to learn something from everyone you meet.

15. Help people be right.

16. Take notes; have a mindset that you will need to send the other person a recap of what he or she said, even if you won't.

WEED YOUR MENTAL GARDEN

Just as weeds will choke out the plants in your garden, mental clutter will choke out the productive thought processes you need to be totally productive. Reduce your mental clutter, and you will get a lot more done.

An important person to help you weed the garden and reduce mental clutter is an assistant. If this isn't an option, perhaps someone can act in that capacity for you. Or, commit the items listed below to writing, get in the habit of scheduling brief meetings with yourself to get and stay organized, and keep important things moving.

The person you designate can handle administrative matters, your schedule, personal organization, and preparation, be someone who "breaks log jams," keeps things moving, fights fires, performs due diligence, and does any research required. Here are some things you can do to fully utilize this person's talents:

1. Identify and communicate your most important goals.
2. Identify and communicate your top five or six high-pay-off activities (priorities).
3. Develop written expectations. These can include:
    a. Handle mail, correspondence, phone calls, and e-mail for you
    b. Maintain your schedule. Be sure to communicate changes ASAP
    c. Handle drop-in visitors using your principles for "degrees of access"
    d. Oversee paper flow
    e. Automatically find/prepare information needed for your tasks or to do's
    f. Respect your personal preferences and idiosyncrasies
4. Hold a briefing meeting each morning with (10-15 minutes). Review the following:
    a. Your schedule, meetings, phone calls, etc.
    b. Projects/to do's
    c. Information/material needed
    d. People he/she needs to contact for you
5. Hold a de-briefing meeting at the end of each day (10-15 minutes). Review the following:
    a. Completed tasks (close the loop)
    b. Incomplete tasks, open issues, and new developments
    c. Decisions and/or help needed

6. Have your assistant provide a written briefing at the end of each day. This can be as succinct or thorough as you want. The key is to keep you informed so you can close all mental loops.

7. When you are traveling, the daily briefing and de-briefing can be done by phone and/or e-mail. The 20 minutes a day invested in these meetings will pay off in increased productivity, improved communication, reduced frustration, and professional growth for both of you.

8. Let your assistant make a case for taking projects/to do's away from you. The tendency to hang on to things is the greatest enemy of weeding the garden and reducing mental clutter.

IDENTIFY AND STAY IN HIGH-PAYOFF ACTIVITIES

High-Payoff Activities (HPA's) are those activities that give you the "biggest bang for the buck." They are activities that help you achieve your goals, pay you and your organization the most, give you the greatest return on your investment of time and other resources, prevent problems, and allow you to fulfill your responsibilities. These activities could include planning; relationship building with employees, customers, vendors and prospects; preparation; crises prevention; and performing the main functions of your job.

If you consistently concentrate on the parts of your work that have the greatest potential instead of paying equal attention to everything and everybody, you will be much more productive. To create priorities and stay in high-payoff activities, ask yourself:

■   Which activities or tasks will give me the greatest return for the amount of time I invest?

- Which activities or tasks, if left undone, will create the biggest threat to the accomplishment of my goals?

- Which activities, tasks, projects, or goals does my boss consider most important?

- Which activities or tasks will best help me reach my intermediate and long-term goals?

- Who or what will suffer if I don't complete one of these tasks or projects today?

- Which items will make me feel the best long-term when I accomplish them?

BALANCE EFFECTIVENESS AND EFFICIENCY

Ask yourself, "If I don't have time to do it right the first time, when will I have time to do it over?"

Effectiveness is best described as doing the right things. Efficiency is best described as doing things right. In most cases, a balance between the two is ideal – do the right things right. Getting the right balance depends on a lot of factors. Knowing what those factors are, in each case, will go a long way toward making sure you have the right balance between effectiveness and efficiency.

OVERCOME PROCRASTINATION

Procrastination is an insidious malady that is the bane of productivity and progress. It can be caused by many things: unclear goals or expectations, lack of confidence, low self-image, lack of feedback, fear of failure, and perfectionism. People tend to avoid unpleasant or difficult jobs or jobs that are too big or too time-consuming.

Whether the cause is internal or external, the solution is to break inertia with action. It is easier to act your way to a new set of feelings than it is to feel your way to a new set of actions.

When you sense that you are procrastinating, you should focus on the payoff. Take some immediate action, such as jot down a note on paper, make a phone call, schedule an action step, make an appointment, or do anything else that will break inertia, including breaking the task into bite-sized chunks. Reward yourself when you take timely action.

OTHER PEOPLE'S TIME --- DELEGATION

Inability to delegate is one of the leading causes of management failure. Reasons given for not delegating effectively include:

- Being too busy. Ironically, this is the one most often cited.

- Not trusting people to complete assignments on time or correctly.

- Having trouble letting go and being a slave to "If you want a job done right, you have to do it yourself."

- Not knowing how to delegate effectively.

Benefits of effective delegation:

- Gets employees more involved.

- Gives you a chance to develop employees.

- Teaches employees to take initiative and be responsible.

- Increases the motivation level and improves morale.

- Multiplies time for achieving results.

Delegation is a people development tool, as well as a time-management tool. Effective delegation increases the self-confidence of those being delegated to and communicates that you believe in them, have confidence in them, and need them to accomplish the team's goals.

Delegation also helps you, the team leader, stay in higher-payoff activities and support all team members better. As you move from "doing" to managing or leading, you become more valuable to the organization. Also, when your employees can handle more responsibility, you are better prepared to accept more responsibilities and opportunities yourself.

BASIC RULES OF DELEGATION

1. Make decisions at the lowest level where necessary information and judgment are present.

2. Have employees bring you solutions, not problems.

3. Delegate, do, or defer.

STEPS TO EFFECTIVE DELEGATION

1. Select people who have the ability to do the job or who can learn.

2. Explain what the job entails and why it is important.

3. Establish reasonable deadlines.

4. State the expected results in measurable terms.

5. Express your confidence in a person's ability to complete the tasks.

6. Reward results appropriately.

7. Resist doing a job that you have delegated.

LEVELS OF DELEGATION

Wait until told what to do

This indicates a low level of confidence in the person performing the work and can be time consuming and unproductive.

Seek permission before acting

There are cases where this is appropriate. You can minimize these with effective training.

Act and report immediately

This shows a higher level of confidence in the person performing the work. However, in many cases it might cause lags in productivity if the supervisor is not readily available when the work is completed. Effective coaching will help develop people at this level move to the highest level.

Act and report routinely

This is the highest level of delegation, empowerment, initiative, and responsibility. It demonstrates confidence in the person performing the work and utilizes time and human resources effectively. By getting the right people in the right positions, having a good training program, and coaching effectively, you can strive to get as many people as possible to this level.

STAY OUT OF THE DRAMA TRIANGLE

In most, if not all, work environments, a lot of time and energy is wasted on drama. The Drama Triangle has three positions: Victim, Persecutor, and Rescuer. If you fall into the Drama Triangle in any of the positions and stay on the triangle long enough, you will end up as the victim.
Victims take the position "Poor me," or "It's not my fault; there is nothing I can do." They will play games such as, "Woe is me," "Ain't it awful," or "If it weren't for…"

They play the role of being hopeless, helpless, and/or powerless. They believe that other people can make them feel good or bad. Victims will have a tendency to look for a Rescuer that will perpetuate their negative feelings.

Drama Triangle

Persecutor
Keeps Victim oppressed
Blames / Criticizes

I can make you feel bad.
It's all your fault!
What were you thinking?
How could you...?

"Drama"
Energy draining
Emotion-laden
Time consuming
Disruptive
Counter-productive
Divisive

Rescuer
Appears nice and helpful
Keeps Victim Dependant
Gives permission to fail

I can make you feel good.
Let me help you.

Victim
Feels Hopeless/Helpless/Powerless
You can make me feel bad or good.
Woe is me.
Ain't it awful!?!
It's not my fault.
There's nothing I can do!
If it weren't for...

Responsibile

What is my responsibilty?
What can I/we learn from this?
What are my/your options?
What would I/you do different next time?

MOTTO: "If there is no wind, row!"

Persecutors take the position, "It's all your fault." They will say things like, "What were you thinking?" or "How could you be so stupid?" They believe, "I can make you feel bad." They set strict limits unnecessarily, blame, criticize, keep victims oppressed, are mobilized by anger, are rigid and authoritative in stance, and are a "critical" parent.

Rescuers take the position, "Let me help you." Their real goal is to keep the Victim dependant. They give Victims permission to fail. They appear to be nice and helpful and they believe, "I can make you feel good."

Once you fall into the triangle, it can be very difficult to get out. Also, as one player shifts positions, other players will shift positions also.

You can stay out of, or get out of, the Drama Triangle by taking a fourth position – outside the triangle. This position is Responsibility. Ask yourself, "What is my responsibility in this situation?" "What can I learn from this?" "What are my options?" or "What would I do different next time?" The Responsibility position could have the motto, "If there is no wind, row."

KEEPING THE MAIN THING THE MAIN THING - SUMMARY

✓ It is essential to create balance in your life and minimize the amount of time you spend rushing through tasks and activities.

✓ Instead of trying to manage your time, focus on doing a better job of managing yourself.

✓ Effective delegation increases the self-confidence of those being delegated to and communicates that you believe in them, have confidence in them, and need them to accomplish the team's goals.

✓ Focus and concentration help you be more productive.

✓ You can stay out of the Drama Triangle by accepting responsibility.

KEEPING THE MAIN THING THE MAIN THING - AFFIRMATIONS

✓ I take time to clear mental clutter.

✓ I stay in high payoff activities by effectively delegating to others.

✓ I avoid multi-tasking and stay in the moment.

✓ I strive for a balance between effectiveness and efficiency.

✓ I accept responsibility and stay outside of the Drama Triangle.

Part IV

Effective Communicator

Day in and day out, we are engaged in communication. Yet, as often as we communicate, effective communication remains a challenging skill to master.

Communication is complex. We can miscommunicate, fail to communicate, or communicate poorly. We can be misheard, mis-understood, or never heard at all. Our communication can be helpful or hurtful.

As a leader, you should continually strive to become an effective communicator. Good communication skills will empower you to build trust, foster learning, and create a motivational environment.

As you will discover throughout the next five chapters, good communication requires an exchange of information. As a leader, it is essential that you both ask better questions, as well as listen effectively to those around you. You will learn how to improve performance through feedback and how using authority appropriately will help you gain commitment from others and ultimately achieve more.

Finally, in the last chapter of this book, we will discuss the effect of integrity on your personal leadership and how it will impact your success. Leadership is a journey. Your completion of this book and implementation of the ideas contained within it are a symbol of your personal commitment to your leadership development.

14.

Bridging the Communication Gap

*"The way we communicate with others and with ourselves
ultimately determines the quality of our lives."*

- Anthony Robbins

*Several years ago, when Ivory soap first came on the market,
an advertising agency was retained to write an ad for Ivory
soap. Two ad writers were given the task.*

Ad writer number one wrote:

*The alkaline elements and fats in this product are blended in
such a way as to secure the highest quality of saponification,
along with the specific gravity that keeps it on top of the water, relieving the bather of the trouble and annoyance of fish-
ing around for it a the bottom of the tub during ablutions.*

Ad writer number two wrote:

It floats.

*Of course, ad writer number two got the job because he com-
municated simply.*

THE NECESSITY OF EXCHANGE

Whenever two or more people make contact, communication occurs. It can occur in person, by phone, through
e-mail, in voice mail, during a video conference, at meetings
or conferences, or at speeches or workshops. Communication is the exchange of thoughts, messages, feelings, goals,

or information. The key word is exchange. Unless an exchange takes place, communication has not occurred.

WHY YOU CANNOT NOT COMMUNICATE

Whether you realize it or not, if you ignore someone, you are participating in a form of negative communication. Poor and no communication can damage your relationships.

Effective communication, on the other hand, can make good relationships great and great relationships extraordinary. Unfortunately, many people assume they are effective communicators so when miscommunications occur, they blame the other person.

Good communication does not happen by accident. It requires an intentional effort and good use of words, phrasing, body language, facial expressions, and listening skills. It is not easy, but it is worth the effort because it improves relationships, performance, and results.

PURPOSES OF INTENTIONAL COMMUNICATION

- » To understand and be understood
- » To get things done and accomplish goals
- » To sell products, services, or a point of view
- » To be more productive
- » To improve teamwork
- » To save time
- » To establish trust and improve relationships
- » To teach and inform
- » To motivate and help people grow
- » To solve problems

Whether you are the sender or receiver in a communication, being an intentional communicator will pay big dividends.

EFFECTIVENESS OF COMMUNICATION

Regardless of the purpose, effective communication needs elements of motivation, stimulation, inspiration, listening, involvement, and evaluation to insure an effective exchange. Just as there can be interference in electronic transmissions, there can be interference in human transmissions. The following formula can be used to describe effective communication:

Communication Formula

Quality of Message
+ Qualifiy of Delivery
- Distractions & Interference
_____
Effective Communication

The quality of the message and delivery, minus the amount of interference, equals the effectiveness of communication. The better the quality of the message and delivery and the least amount of interference insures the best possible communication.

The quality of the message is determined by the words you use and how you phrase them. People think in "word pictures," and most words have many different meanings. Therefore, the meaning of words lies within people – their experiences and memory bank. Choose your words carefully and phrase them in terms of the other person.

The quality of the delivery is determined by the tone

and inflection you use, your facial expressions, and your body language. Make sure your tone, inflection, facial expressions, and body language are congruent with your message.

Even when the quality of your message and delivery is good, you still need to be concerned about the following interference and distortion factors.

INTERFERENCE AND DISTORTION FACTORS

» Word choice – what you say.

» Tone and inflection – how you say it.

» Body language and facial expression – how you look.

» Your mannerisms – how you act.

» Not revealing ALL the information. This can be deliberate or caused by lack of attention to details.

» Improper preparation or presentation for the intended audience.

» Not gaining, or keeping, the receiver's full attention; not breaking the receiver's pre-occupation.

» External clutter (noise and other distractions).

» The receiver's emotional or mental baggage.

» Differences in social, cultural, economic, or educational backgrounds.

» Technology glitches, such as e-mails going into "cyberspace," illegible faxes, poor phone reception, etc.

Fortunately, most of the factors that affect communication can be controlled or compensated by you. You can choose and control your words, tone and inflection, body language, and facial expressions. You can compensate for different environments and culture, experience, and knowledge differences. You can learn about other people in order to gauge the differences in experience and knowledge.

In most communication situations, words represent approximately 7 percent of the total communication, tone and inflection 38 percent, and body language 55 percent. This means if you are not communicating face-to-face, you lose 55 percent of your effectiveness.

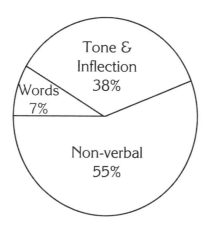

Also, the most commonly used words in the English language can have several meanings. Choosing your words carefully, using tone of voice and inflection wisely, and asking for feedback regularly are critical for effective communication, especially if the conversations are not in person.

BARRIERS TO EFFECTIVE COMMUNICATION

Communicating effectively is a learned skill that will take time to develop. As a leader, it is important that you both recognize and learn to overcome the barriers that may stand in your way as you develop effective communication skills.

Attitude

People assume that others will do what they would do in a similar circumstance, but that is not always the case. Usually, people will do things for their reasons, not yours. Observe people. Watch what they are interested in and what they pay attention to. Keen observation provides you with insight and knowledge on how to communicate effectively with people who have different interests or use a different communication style.

Lack of trust

The key is to build trust with other people one encounter at a time.

Relevance

If the person or group you want to communicate with is not interested in the subject you want to discuss or are not on the same page as you, effective communication will be difficult to achieve.

Values

People have different values, but this should not deter you from having effective communication. The key to effective communication is knowing what the values are and respecting any differences.

Words

The 500 most commonly used words in the English language have more than 15,000 meanings. People think in word pictures. When you say a word, people form an image of what they think you mean. If their picture is different than yours, miscommunication is likely. Choose your words carefully and encourage feedback and questions for clarification.

Tone and inflection

The way you say something has a powerful effect on how words are received. You might think you are communicating calmly and clearly, yet the recipient may think you are being vague and terse. Think about what you want other people to know, think, or do, and choose your tone and inflection accordingly.

Body language and facial expression
People typically believe what they see over what they hear. Make sure your body language and facial expressions are congruent with your intended message. When you are relaxed, confident, and speaking with honesty and integrity, your body language and facial expressions will more than likely be congruent with your message.

HOW TO AVOID MISCOMMUNICATIONS

Someone sent an e-mail to a government bureau asking whether hydrochloric acid could be used to clean the tubes in a steam boiler.

He received this reply from the government bureau, "Uncertainty of reactive processes make the use of hydrochloric acid undesirable where alkalinity is involved."

The man wrote back, "Thanks for the advice; I'll start using it tomorrow."

Back from Washington came this urgent message, "Regrettable decision involved certain uncertainties. Hydrochloric acid will produce sublimate invalidating reactions."

He replied, "Thanks again. Glad to know it's ok."

This time there came this urgent and clear message, "Don't use hydrochloric acid. It will eat out your tubes."

Miscommunications create unnecessary problems, misunderstandings, hurt feelings, confused instructions, loss of important information, embarrassment, frustration, and lost opportunities.

The biggest miscommunication is to assume communication has taken place. How many times have you been disappointed by someone you thought understood you, only to find out they were on a different page than you? In the movie, "Cool Hand Luke," the warden kept saying about Luke, "What we have here is a failure to communicate." The warden assumed it was Luke's fault and did not shoulder any of the responsibility. This happens tens of thousands of times every day in business and personal relationships. People can get used to poor communication and accept it as a natural part of life. It doesn't have to be that way.

To reduce miscommunications, missed expectations, frustrations, confusion, disappointments, anger, and many other emotions, consider the following when you are attempting to communicate:

Know what your goal is
What do you want the other person to know, think, and/or do?

Choose your words carefully
Words set the parameters of how people will react to you. If possible, practice what you are going to say and/or write out what you want to say. Gauge the level of your words and language to the level of the recipient.

Use the proper tone and inflection
Emphasizing different words in a sentence can dramatically change the way your message is perceived.

Make certain your body language and facial expressions are congruent with your message
If you tell someone they did a good job but roll your eyes as you say it, what are they going to believe – your words or your facial expression? People believe what they see over what they hear every time!

Observe the body language and facial expressions of the person with whom you are communicating
You can pick up invaluable clues about the effectiveness of your communication and gauge how well your message is being received by observing body language and facial expressions.

Pace yourself to the mental speed of your listener
Regardless of intelligence, some people process information faster than others. You can usually tell how fast a person processes information by how fast he or she talks. Pace yourself accordingly. If you are going to err, err on the side of speaking just a little slower than the other person.

Actively ask for feedback
Ask an open-ended question such as, "So we can be sure we are communicating effectively, would you tell me your understanding of what we just discussed?" If you are on the same page or wavelength, move on. If not, clarify and discuss the topic until you are. Avoid questions such as: "Do you understand?", "Have I made myself clear?", or "Do you hear what I'm saying?" Such closed-end questions can cause your listener to give you a tacit "yes," or worse yet, make them feel as if you think they are stupid, which can lead to a communication shutdown.

Control the environment as much as possible
If there is a lot of noise or other distractions, move to a quieter location with fewer distractions.

Ask questions
Continue to inquire until you get to the heart of the matter or accomplish your goal. The answers are in the questions. The better your questions, the better the answers and results.

Listen
Ineffective listening can be the greatest cause of miscommunications in every area of life. In business, when employees

do not feel heard by management, they frequently complain to co-workers, family, and friends. Venting feelings of frustration can take on epidemic proportions in the workplace. On the other hand, effective listening can be the primary reason for meaningful communication. Careful listening is difficult and takes practice to improve, but it is worth the time and effort it takes to improve it.

HOW TO IMPROVE COMMUNICATION

To get people to change what they are doing, you have to change what they are thinking. To change what they are thinking, you have to change what you are saying and, perhaps, how you are saying it. Listed below are several techniques for improving communication:

Break pre occupation
Never assume that because people are physically in the same room with you that they are mentally with you. They might have come directly from another meeting to meet with you, be focused on a serious problem, or have pressing matters that need their attention. One of the best techniques for breaking pre occupation is to ask a relatively easy-to-answer, open-ended question that will make people think before responding.

Establish rapport
If this person is not someone you communicate with on a regular basis, look for something you have in common. Perhaps talking about a hobby or other interest, education, a sports team, a civic organization, or other experiences could break the ice for communication.

Establish credibility
If you do not have it already, you must earn the trust of people to communicate clearly.

Have an agenda for the meeting
Even if it is a short, stand-up meeting, it is important to clarify your goals and expectations and establish priorities.

Relax
Be relaxed, positive, and confident. If you appear nervous, on edge, or uptight, people may mimic your behavior, or it could make them uncomfortable.

Be, and stay, in the moment
Years ago, a co-worker of mine requested that when he and I talked that I treat him as if he was the only person I worked with. This lesson has been invaluable to me as I have learned to be and stay in the moment regardless of what else I may have going on. Wherever you are, be there.

Value people
Never look up or down to anyone and do not take people for granted. They will feel it and resent you for it, thus reducing your ability to effectively communicate.

Respect differences in personalities and style
Realize that all people are important and have something to share. Many times it is the differences that create synergy or give meaning to a relationship.

Take time to communicate effectively
Most communication problems can be solved when both parties make a commitment to maintain a dialogue until the problem is solved. The next time you have a serious communication challenge, use Stephen Covey's technique: "This issue is too important to me to not resolve it. I'm willing to take as long as necessary to reach a satisfactory conclusion. Are you? Great. Why don't you go first?"

Inspect what you expect
Follow up on important communication situations to make certain the appropriate information has been conveyed, is

being applied, and is being acted upon. People respect you when you inspect what you expect.

THE ROLE OF WORDS, QUESTIONS, AND PHRASING

Words and phrasing are important to the interpretation of the message you are delivering. A statement phrased differently will have a different understanding and, as a result, a different reaction.

For example, you could say to the special person in your life, "When I look into your eyes, time stands still." Most likely, this statement, delivered to the appropriate person, will have a positive reaction. However, phrasing this statement slightly differently by saying, "Your face would stop a clock." will earn you a negative response and probably lead to hurt feelings and a damaged relationship.

Questions, in addition to phrasing, play an important role in our communication. When worded correctly, questions will arouse interest, encourage the other person to talk, help clarify thoughts, and gather information such as what the other person wants and why they want it. Questions will also help you gain control or stay in control of the conversation and change the subject when it is necessary. Also, when you ask someone a question, particularly if it is for their opinion, it creates a psychological reciprocity and builds trust.

Ask yourself a few questions in order to develop a series of effective questions:

What does the other person REALLY want?

What is the other person FEELING?

What is the other person THINKING?

What are the other person's GOALS?

What BENEFITS does the person want to GAIN?

What LOSSES does the person want to AVOID?

What POINT is the person trying to make?

What are the FACTS in the situation?

What ACTION does the person want you to take?

WHO influences this person?

WHAT is important to this person?

To help ensure the questions you are asking are effective, be sure to:

- Phrase questions in terms of output wanted.

- Move from general and easy-to-answer questions to more difficult open-ended questions.

- Never assume people have answered your question. Drill down by asking second- and third-level questions.

- Put other people at ease. If you are relaxed, other people will feel more comfortable responding to your questions.

- Be friendly and sincere rather than combative and adversarial. Learn to control your body language and facial expressions, especially when you might be tense or in a stressful situation.

- Keep your questions brief, specific, and easy to understand. Avoid asking multiple questions at one time.

- Be patient. Give the other person time to respond.

- Watch as well as listen to every response.

- Ask questions with the understanding that the answer given will be an idea, action step, behavior change, and/or goal.

BRIDGING THE COMMUNICATION GAP - SUMMARY

✓ Communication is the exchange of thoughts, messages, feelings, goals, or information.

✓ The quality of the message and delivery, minus the amount of interference, equals the effectiveness of communication.

✓ Effective communication can make good relationships great and great relationships extraordinary.

✓ If you are not communicating face-to-face, you lose 55 percent of your effectiveness.

✓ The biggest miscommunication is to assume communication has taken place.

BRIDGING THE COMMUNICATION GAP - AFFIRMATIONS

✓ I am a good communicator.

✓ I choose my words carefully.

✓ I am a good listener.

✓ I never assume communication has taken place.

✓ I ask one question at a time.

15.
Asking Questions and Listening

"The answers are in the questions. If you want better answers, ask better questions."

- John G. Miller

For the first eight years of our marriage, my wife and I had an unplanned and unrehearsed ritual. Every Sunday afternoon, she would be preparing dinner, and I would be watching my favorite sporting event on TV.

As my hunger pangs grew, I would ask my wife, "When will dinner be ready?" Her response was always, "As soon as the potatoes are done." to which I would respond, "O.K."

Although I responded, I truly had no idea when dinner would actually be ready. Eventually I realized that if I wanted a different answer, I needed to ask a different question.

THE ANSWERS ARE IN THE QUESTIONS

If you want better answers, you need to ask better questions. Questions can be used to gather information, identify and solve problems, get feedback, improve performance, determine results, and facilitate coaching, counseling, confronting, or disciplining. The better you get at asking the right questions, the better you will be at getting the results you want.

Closed-end questions can be answered with "yes" or "no" or a single word. Answers to closed-end questions are usually short and specific. The answer to "Did you complete your report?" will most likely be a yes or no. The answer to "What time is the meeting?" will be a specific time. The answer to "How many people were at the meeting?" will be a specific number or an estimate. "Where did you buy your computer" will generate a specific location.

Closed-end questions are good conversation starters. By asking closed-end, easy to answer questions, you put the other person at ease and get a conversation started. The answers to these questions can give you information that will prompt an opportunity to ask open-end questions. Closed-end questions can also be good conversation "closers." Scheduling an appointment is one example of using a closed-end question to end a conversation.

Open-end questions, on the other hand, are "thinking, feeling, finding" questions. They usually produce longer answers and more insight into what the other person is thinking or feeling. Open-end questions will reveal the emotion behind the answers and give you a lot more information into the other person's state of mind. They are questions that encourage people to talk about whatever is important to them because they help gather information, establish rapport, and increase understanding. If you ask an open-end question, you should be ready and willing to listen to the response.

Examples of open-end questions include: "How can I be of help?", "Would you tell me more about _____?", "Could you help me understand _____?", "What are some of the things you've tried?", "What do you mean?", "How do you feel about that?"

TYPES OF QUESTIONS

WHO	Used to identify people	'Who are the possible candidates?"
WHERE	Used to establish or identify a location	"Where can you find the information?"
WHAT	Used to identify activities or objectives	"What's the next step?"
WHEN	Used to identify a time or date	"When will you decide?"
WHY	Used to identify the reason, purpose, goal, or cause	"Why is that important to you?"
HOW	Used to cause thought, identify steps, or solve a problem	"How do you measure productivity?"

As a general rule, men and women use language differently. In unfamiliar or stressful situations, men tend to prefer to use and respond to closed-end questions. Women tend to prefer open-end questions. The better you know the other person, the easier it will be to choose the appropriate questions.

A WORD OF CAUTION

Sometimes even the most well-intentioned, perfectly phrased question can illicit a negative or defensive response. Most people are good at answering questions, but some individuals can perceive questions as threatening or intimidating. Perhaps the person had a domineering boss or parent who used questions as a means of placing blame or as a means of punishment.

A well-phrased statement can be a good substitute for a question. A statement can open the door for the other person's response. A statement does not require a reply and will usually be perceived as less threatening than many questions. Instead of challenging people with questions that might be perceived as threatening, make statements that elicit a voluntary reply.

"I can imagine there are a number of possible solutions to that problem" is a statement that could get the other person to voluntarily submit some possible solutions.

How a question or statement is framed can largely determine what the majority of people will decide and actually do.

AVOIDING MISCOMMUNICATIONS

As Stephen Covey says, "To be trusted, we must be trustworthy or worthy of trust." One of the most important things you can do to avoid miscommunications is be trustworthy. Receivers are more likely to believe your message if they trust you and are confident you have their best interest in mind.

To avoid miscommunications, use simple, easy to understand words. Most people are not impressed by individuals who use large, uncommonly used words and complex language. Use the language the listener is most likely to understand. Instead of "make an alteration" to a report, tell them to "change" it. Don't ask them to "render assistance," ask them to "help." Instead of "have a discussion," use "talk."

You should also make certain your expectations,

goals, and performance standards are clearly defined and understood; always be specific when indicating deadlines. Telling someone "when you get a chance" diminishes urgency and fails to set a completion date.

When engaged in face-to-face conversation, make sure your body language and facial expression are congruent with your words; otherwise, your receiver will get a mixed message and communication will be incomplete.

Before sending an e-mail or letter that could possibly be misunderstood, read it aloud or have a trusted confidant read it first. Likewise, before leaving a voice message that might cause a problem if it is misunderstood, use the review option before sending the message.

If you are sending an e-mail from a wireless device, include a tag line so people know why your answer is terse.

In written communication, state clearly what you want the other person to do, e.g. read it, take action, file it, respond, etc.

In all forms of communication, it is vital to stay in the moment. The human brain can think four to five times faster than most people speak. This phenomenon will cause gaps and your brain will search for other things to do, e.g. think about what you are going to do after work, or look for solutions to a problem you've been working on, or think about what you are going to say next. Train your brain to stay in the moment. You can do this by taking good notes, or asking clarifying questions, making eye contact, removing distractions, etc.

If it is apparent to you that the other person is pre-occupied or otherwise not paying full attention to you and your message, either do something to gain his or her full attention or schedule a time when you can have his or her full attention. Break pre occupation or don't attempt to communicate.

Always remember to treat other people with dignity and respect. When you rant and rave, yell, lose your temper, or use superlatives, the other person will tend to get tense, receptors in his or her brain will shut down, and communication will be limited, at best.

To ensure continual improvement, ask people you communicate with on a regular basis what you can do to communicate better and then do it.

THE ROLE OF ACTIVE LISTENING

Listening involves more than your ears. It involves your eyes and any other senses you can put into play. When you see what a person pays attention to, you can tell what their intentions are. Listen to the words they use. Watch their facial expressions and body language. What is important to them? Are they using contradictory terms or phrases? Are they avoiding answering certain questions or skirting certain issues? Are they making eye contact? All of these are signals you can interpret to help you communicate. This is called active listening. Think of listening as a precious gift you are giving the other person. Even in the most difficult situations, people appreciate it when you listen.

People Fail to Hear Because They Are:

- Too busy preparing what they are going to say
- Letting their mind wander (We listen at least four times faster than we speak.)
- Lazy (It takes effort to listen effectively.)
- Faking attention
- Egotistical or mentally set (They lack interest in what other people are saying.)
- Impatient

To Encourage Others to Talk:

Be quiet
Will Rogers said, "Never miss a good opportunity to shut up." Most people have a favorite topic – themselves.

Be sincerely interested in what other people are saying
People can sense insincerity and they will resent it.

Encourage people with supportive nods and phrases
"Uh-huh," "I see," "That's interesting," etc.

Guide the conversation with questions
Remember, the question mark is mightier than the exclamation point.

Avoid interrupting other people
Interrupting is a form of disrespect.

Concentrate on what other people are trying to say
Pay attention to their words, ideas, and feelings related to the subject.

Make eye contact
Position yourself so it will be easy to make frequent eye contact.

Stay in the moment
Compartmentalize any other issues that might distract you.

Get rid of distractions
Put down papers or pencils, unless you are taking notes. Turn off your cell phone or put it on silent mode. Turn your computer monitor off or close your laptop.

Ask for clarification if you do not understand a point or idea
Don't assume you understand. When you ask a question, it shows you are interested in what the other person is saying and helps ensure your understanding.

Keep in mind that it is hard to get away from a good

listener. People will think you are brilliant when you let them talk about the most important person in their life (them) or things they are interested in.

LEVELS OF LISTENING

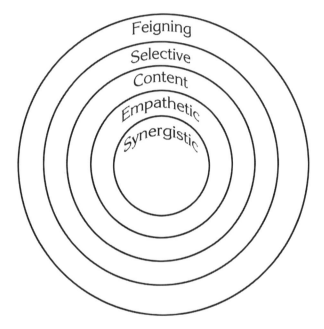

At the lowest level, people listen to the words and are not really paying attention. This is the Feigning Level. The fake listener does not fool most people. Poor eye contact, busy hands, and meaningless replies give them away. This is rude and a waste of the speaker's and listener's time.

Next is the Selective Level. People at this level listen to the words and hear what they want to hear. These people are not open to what is new or what they can learn. This can be an automatic reaction that causes people to miss opportunities to learn.

The third level is known as the Content Level. At this level, people are open to hearing the facts. However, they usually interpret what the other person means without clarifying with them what they really meant. This self-assessment can lead to miscommunications.

The Empathetic Level follows the Content Level. At this level, the listener is able to listen from the other person's point of view, which helps them feel understood. This will create a situation where they will want to reciprocate. Listening at this level requires that you understand not only the content of the information, but the intent. Listening with sincere interest conveys respect and makes the other person feel appreciated.

The Synergistic Level is the highest level and focuses on areas of alignment, leverage, and synergy. It can lead to high levels of learning and can create opportunities for collaboration. This level is where relationships are solidified and enhanced.

The richest personal benefits and best results come from the Empathetic and Synergistic Levels. As a result, you should strive to spend the majority of your time in these two levels.

BENEFITS OF ACTIVE LISTENING

- Prevents misunderstandings.
- Improves insight into people's wants and needs.
- Enhances relationships.
- Increases opportunities to learn.
- Reduces friction and resolves conflict.
- Enlists support and favorable response.
- Encourages a more honest and sincere exchange.

ASKING QUESTIONS AND LISTENING - SUMMARY

✓ Questions can be used to gather information, identify and solve problems, get feedback, improve performance, determine results, and facilitate coaching, counseling, confronting, or disciplining.

✓ A well-phrased statement can be a good substitute for a question.

✓ To avoid miscommunications, use simple, easy to understand words.

✓ When engaged in face-to-face conversation, make sure your body language and facial expression are congruent with your words.

✓ Listening involves your eyes and any other senses you can put into play.

ASKING QUESTIONS AND LISTENING - AFFIRMATIONS

✓ I ask the right questions to get the answers I need.

✓ I am a good listener.

✓ I am trustworthy.

✓ I treat others with dignity and respect.

✓ I stay in the moment when listening to others.

16.
Improving Performance with Feedback

"Encouragement is the oxygen of the soul."

- George M. Adams

During a workshop recently, I asked participants to tell me how long they could live without air.

"Minutes," replied several individuals.

"How long could you survive without water?" I asked.

"Days," someone said.

I inquired again, asking, "How long can you live without food?"

"Weeks," they shouted.

And finally, I asked, "How long can you live without feedback?"

"Forever," they agreed.

"Not true," I responded.

"Whether we realize it or not, we are constantly receiving feedback from the environment around us. We feel the sun on our backs. We see the expressions on people's faces. We hear the sound of a child crying. Feedback is constant. It is everywhere and it is impossible to live without it.

"So how long can we really live without feedback," I asked again?

"Moments."

THE ROLE OF POSITIVE REINFORCEMENT

People need feedback to validate their existence, enhance their self-esteem, and improve their self-image. One of the greatest forms of punishment in prison is solitary confinement because it has little or no feedback. People's self-images are developed by the feedback they get from experiences and/or other people.

Feedback is important if you want to improve individual performance and team productivity. Giving appropriate feedback is the quickest, cheapest, and most effective method for improving performance and results.

All feedback affects people's behavior in one way or another. Our reaction to feedback or lack of feedback shapes our lives.

Twin brothers were interviewed separately on their 60th birthday. The reporter noted that one of the brothers was an alcoholic, and the other was a total abstainer. When the alcoholic brother was asked about his use of alcohol, he replied that his father was an alcoholic, and that is why he was. His twin responded that his father was an alcoholic, and that is why he abstained.

The same stimulus produced two different responses. It isn't what happens to us that counts; it is our reaction to what happens to us that counts.

THE ABSENCE OF FEEDBACK

The dilemma with feedback in business is that most people won't ask for feedback, and most business leaders don't give enough appropriate feedback. Most people will not ask for feedback because they do not want to appear weak or to be perceived as "high maintenance." They may also think that if they have to ask for feedback, it is not valuable.

Leaders don't give enough appropriate feedback for many reasons, including:

- They do not fully understand the value and importance.

- They do not know how.

- They do not think they have enough time because they are too busy.

- They do not get enough from their coach.

- They have had poor role models in the past.

When people have to guess what they are supposed to do it creates tension, and they won't do their best work. Avoid telling people to "do their best". What does "do your best" mean? What does "try harder" mean? What does a "comprehensive report" look like?

Sometimes workers know they are doing things they should not be doing, but they don't realize it is a problem. To avoid this, ask:

How do you know when you are doing a good or bad job?

How do you measure the quality of your performance?

How do you know when you do something wrong?

Describe what good performance looks like.

Describe what bad performance looks like.

When people clearly understand what is expected of them, it reduces the relationship tension and improves their ability to perform up to your expectations.

TYPES OF FEEDBACK

Positive feedback causes people to repeat the behavior. When people teach young children to walk, talk, learn the alphabet, read, write, ride a bicycle, or anything else, they use lots of positive feedback. This encourages children to repeat the behavior, builds on their successes, and improves their self-esteem. Parents and teachers need a lot of patience to encourage children to accomplish desired goals. Effective leaders also need to use positive feedback to get adults to perform in a manner that will accomplish the desired goals of the organization.

Negative feedback causes people to do only what is necessary to avoid punishment. People tend to become totally subjected to negative feedback – for example, they will only do what they are told so they can avoid negative feedback, or they become immune to it and will only do what is necessary to avoid it.

No feedback can be worse than negative feedback. No feedback is perceived as ignoring people. When you ignore people, they may think you don't like them, approve of them, respect them, or appreciate them or their efforts. Worse yet, they might think you are mad at them. None of these thoughts are rational or constructive, and the net result is poor performance, caused by stress, tension, frustration, and strained relationships. When people are doing well, they want you to notice. If they are doing something wrong or sub-standard, they want to know so they can repair it. Either way, they want and need feedback.

Not giving feedback is a serious breach of a leader's responsibility. In sports, players get feedback after every attempt and frequent feedback from teammates and coaches. Unfortunately, in business, no feedback is often the most frequent type of feedback. Is it any wonder that people are more motivated about their chosen sport or hobby than they are about their profession?

TYPE OF FEEDBACK	OUTCOME
Positive	BUILDS
Negative	DESTROYS
None	DISRESPECTS

BENEFITS OF EFFECTIVE FEEDBACK

Improves motivation and morale

People who receive appropriate feedback feel good about themselves; people who feel good about themselves are more motivated and have higher morale.

Encourages attendance and employee retention

When people are motivated and have high morale, they want to come to work, they arrive on time, and they stay with the organization longer.

Enhances hiring and recruiting

Motivated employees will tell friends, neighbors, and family members about the great place where they work. This "word of mouth" advertising will help you find better employees when you have a vacancy or expansion in your organization.

Promotes quality

Happy, motivated employees take more pride in their work, make fewer mistakes, and tend to do things right the first time.

Improves customer service and retention

Happy, motivated employees want to do a good job for the customer, and the customers feel it and appreciate it. These happy customers are less likely to complain or take their business elsewhere.

Improves productivity

Happy, motivated employees perform better, which leads to improved productivity.

When I was 11 years old, a Sunday school teacher told me I was a good reader. I believed her and have been an avid reader for the past 50 years, reading 50 plus business books a year. Did feedback affect my self-image and behavior? Absolutely!

PRINCIPLES OF EFFECTIVE FEEDBACK

Consistent

People will perform better for someone who is consistent than they will for someone who is erratic with their feedback. People are more relaxed and will do better work when they know what to expect. When they know they will get positive feedback for good performance, they are more likely to give you good performance. When they know that instructive feedback will focus on improving their performance without retribution, they will be more open to feedback.

Fair

Most people have a wide "fairness streak." If you mistreat an employee or show favoritism, most people resent it, even if it does not happen to them. As a result, they might begin to discount your feedback and possibly lose respect for you.

Frequent

Different people need different amounts and frequency of feedback. It is mainly up to the coach to determine how much feedback each employee needs and how frequently they need it. The amount and frequency usually changes as someone grows in a job or task. For example, when I was coaching a fourth grade girl's basketball team, I would give some of the girls feedback when they dribbled the ball twice in a row without it rolling off the court or when they hit the backboard or rim. As their skill level and confidence grew, they still needed frequent feedback, but for different reasons and at different intervals.

Specific
It is relatively easy to give general feedback such as, "Good job," "Way to go," and "Thanks." With a little more effort, you can be specific and have a far greater impact and result. Some examples of specific feedback could include:

"I was really impressed and pleased with your obvious preparation for today's meeting and the way you addressed the key issues and answered everyone's questions. Thanks!"

"Your idea for adding the shim to the ring assembly will result in fewer returns and happier customers. Good job. Thanks!"

Taking a few extra seconds of time to think about how to be more specific with your feedback will pay big dividends in the way people respond to your feedback and improve their performance.

Avoid showing impatience, annoyance, or anger
Showing impatience, annoyance, or anger can cause tension in a relationship, create stress, and retard performance. Each time I was learning a new stroke in tennis, my instructor showed incredible patience with my lack of grasping the concept or executing the stroke. He never showed annoyance or anger because I wasn't learning as fast as he thought I should. If he had showed annoyance or anger, I probably would have found a different tennis instructor. Employees don't always feel that they have the same luxury. When you show impatience, annoyance, or anger, some will "fire" you by quitting, and some will "fire" you by not performing ef-

fectively.

Someone once described a business associate as "sighing at 90 decibels." He was very bright and was right most of the time. However, if he was watching someone perform badly, his impatience, annoyance, and/or anger would show in a "90 decibel sigh" that was almost as damaging as a temper tantrum.

Don't hold grudges

Holding a grudge hurts the "grudgor" more than the "grudgee." However, grudges hurt relationships, and ineffective relationships limit performance and hinder productivity.

Objective

Base feedback on what is really happening, not what you think is happening, or what you would like to happen. Give feedback based on facts, not on rumors, innuendos, or incomplete information.

Avoid too much pre occupation with your own self interests

When you are pre occupied with your own self interests, it is difficult to focus on someone else and their needs. Be "in the moment" when you are giving feedback. Concentrate on other people and their needs.

Help others whenever possible

There is an old saying, "When you help someone get to the top of a mountain, you'll get there also." The law of reciprocity is free to work when you help other people. You will receive more help when you need it, not necessarily from those you helped.

Don't take yourself too seriously

One of the greatest assets of high achievers is a sense of humor. That does not mean they are good at telling jokes. It means they do not take themselves too seriously. As a result, people are more relaxed around them and find it easier to produce at higher levels.

Be cordial

It does not take much of an effort to be nice to people, and you will feel better, and so will they. People notice when you are nice to other people, even when there is no obvious benefit. When people see you as a friendly person, they are more likely to follow your lead.

Give others the benefit of the doubt

It is easy to be judgmental but often difficult to give people the benefit of the doubt. Judging people can lead to pre judgment, and pre judgment can lead to prejudice. All of us have a strong need to be right. Unfortunately, the need to be right can get in the way of getting what we want. If someone does not do something exactly as you would, give them the benefit of the doubt and show your faith in their abilities.

Giving appropriate feedback is a skill that can be developed like any other skill. Set a goal to improve the quality and quantity of feedback you give. Remind yourself of how important feedback is, reward yourself as you make progress, and practice, practice, practice.

HOW TO GIVE CORRECTIVE FEEDBACK... CORRECTLY

A common misconception is that corrective or informative feedback is negative. This could not be further from the truth. If someone is doing something wrong, they want to know that it is wrong and how to change it. Therefore, when a caring coach gives a performer feedback on an incorrect or inappropriate behavior and information on how to correct it, it should be a positive experience for the performer. The key is to focus on the behavior and desired results, and avoid criticism, sarcasm, annoyance, anger, or impatience.

BUT...AND

Eliminate "but" from your vocabulary. From early childhood, most people are conditioned to hear that they did something right, BUT they also did something wrong. It is a reflex action to wait for the "but" and discount the positive feedback. It might take a few repetitions to get people to stop waiting for the "but," and it will be worth it. If corrective feedback is necessary, handle it at a different time, if possible.

THE ROLE OF SCOREKEEPING IN FEEDBACK

Feedback is most effective when it is specific and based on reality. Unless the coach and player have a method for keeping score and measuring progress, it will be difficult to give appropriate feedback and enjoy improved performance. Therefore, it is crucial to have a method for keeping score and measuring progress. It can be as simple as something you keep on a 3x5 index card or as comprehensive as a computerized document.

IMPROVING PERFORMANCE WITH FEEDBACK - SUMMARY

✓ Giving appropriate feedback is the quickest, cheapest, and most effective method for improving performance and results.

✓ Positive feedback causes people to repeat the behavior.

✓ Giving appropriate feedback is a skill that can be developed like any other skill.

✓ When giving corrective feedback, focus on the behavior

and desired results, and avoid criticism, sarcasm, annoyance, anger, or impatience.

✓ Feedback is most effective when it is specific and based on reality.

IMPROVING PERFORMANCE WITH FEEDBACK - AFFIRMATIONS

✓ I am committed to delivering appropriate feedback.

✓ I am open to receiving and implementing feedback.

✓ I deliver specific feedback.

✓ I have stopped holding grudges.

✓ I eliminated "but" from my feedback.

17.

Using Authority and Influence Wisely

"The key to successful leadership today is influence,
not authority."

- Kenneth Blanchard

The story goes that sometime, close to a battlefield over 200 years ago, a man in civilian clothes rode past a small group of exhausted battle-weary soldiers digging an obviously important defensive position. The section leader, making no effort to help, was shouting orders, threatening punishment if the work was not completed within the hour.

"Why are you are not helping?" asked the stranger on horseback.

"I am in charge. The men do as I tell them," said the section leader, adding, "Help them yourself if you feel strongly about it."

To the section leader's surprise, the stranger dismounted and helped the men until the job was finished.

Before leaving, the stranger congratulated the men for their work and approached the puzzled section leader.

"You should notify top command next time your rank prevents you from supporting your men - and I will provide a more permanent solution," said the stranger.

Up close, the section leader now recognized General Washington and also the lesson he'd just been taught.

AUTHORITY AND INFLUENCE

Authority and influence play important, yet different roles in leadership. In personal leadership, influence is always a factor. However, authority is usually only a factor in formal leadership positions.

Authority is the right to decide no and the right to say yes. Authority can and must be delegated. In addition, you should strive to clarify its limits. If someone has the right to decide either yes or no, but not both, they do not have authority. They have the illusion of authority. Empowering someone to decide no, but not yes, can limit performance and productivity.

Influence is the ability to get people to cooperate because it is in their best interest to do so. In order to influence people, you need to know what motivates them. To know what motivates them, you need to get to know them as a person. The way you get to know them is to ask questions and listen to their responses.

A common misconception is that authority is bestowed and that control and power come with authority. As a result, most people overestimate the amount of control or power they have and tend to underestimate how much they can influence outcomes.

Reality is, titles are usually bestowed, but authority must be earned. You don't need a title to be a leader.

POWER

Power is the capacity to grant and withhold cooperation. Oftentimes as a leader, there is a job to get done that you cannot do alone. If you cannot do it alone, you will need the cooperation of others. Therefore, anyone whose cooperation is needed has power. If a manager had both authority and power, everyone would cooperate automatically to get the job done.

A management problem arises when those with power (employees) refuse to cooperate. Attempts to gain cooperation with authority usually result in bribery or intimidation. If either of these methods worked, most managers would not be needed.

Traditionally, power is based on:

1. Position, rank, and status
2. Knowledge, mastery, and expertise
3. Interpersonal persuasiveness, credibility, and charisma

Most managers tend to over-rely on the areas listed above and under-utilize the real power – their personal power. Personal power is the most enduring power. It is dependant on our own choice and determination to deliberately change our own behaviors, lives, and circumstances to achieve our goals. When we have identified our strengths, know where we stand, where we are going, and how we are going to get there, and have the attitude "if it's to be, it's up to me", we are more likely to use our personal power to persuade others to do what needs to be done to achieve common goals.

THREE TYPES OF CONTROL

1. **Total control** – we have total control over ourselves, e.g. how we look, how we act, what we say, and how we say it.

2. **Partial control** – we have partial control over some people based on our position or authority.

3. **Influence** – most people think the third type of control is no control or "out of control." We have the opportunity to influence many things, and we tend to overestimate

the benefits of total or partial control and underestimate our ability to influence an outcome. The next time you think you do not have any control over a situation or outcome, think about ways you can influence it.

THE PROPER USE OF AUTHORITY

Develop trust
It's not automatically given; it must be earned. Be a person of integrity. Say what you are going to do and do what you say. Treat people fairly and with dignity and respect.

Openly communicate more than you have to or need to
Make it your top priority. Communication, like nature, abhors a vacuum. In the absence of communication, people will create their own messages, typically in the form of rumor, innuendo, and gossip.

Be as specific as possible in the words and phrases you use
Most conflicts and controversies are caused by people not understanding one another. When you use specific, easy to understand words and phrases, you increase the likelihood of being understood.

Supply whatever background information and reasons people need to understand changes
General George S. Patton said, "Never tell people how to do things. Tell them what to do, and why, and they will surprise you with their ingenuity." When you introduce change, make sure people understand why the changes are being made.

Be absolutely honest
If you lie, or sugar coat the truth, your credibility will be destroyed and, remember, the truth will always find you out.

Actively share information
One of the strongest motivators for people is to be "in on

things." Hoarding information doesn't give you power, sharing it does.

Talk to people as one adult to another (the way you would like people to talk with you)

Even if people act like children, resist the temptation to treat them like children. People will live up or down to your expectations. When you treat people like adults, they are more likely to act in a mature way. When you are condescending toward people or treat them with disdain, they will feel it and resent you for it.

Solicit ideas, suggestions, and reactions

Everybody wants to feel important. Everybody can feel important when somebody understands and believes in them. It doesn't take much effort to make people feel important. Little things, done deliberately, at the right time, can make a big difference. Soliciting ideas, suggestions, and reactions will not only make people feel important, you might be surprised at what you learn.

Follow through, always - no exceptions

As a leader, you are on stage all the time. If you don't follow through, or if you drop the ball, you can expect other people to do the same thing.

Recognize that your job is to remove roadblocks, irritants, and frustrations - not put them there

You need others as much or more than they need you. When you remove roadblocks, irritants, and frustrations, you help others become successful, and you will be more successful also.

The proper use of authority will influence the people whose cooperation is needed to accomplish the tasks that must be completed in order to achieve your goals.

THE ROLE OF ACTIVE LISTENING IN INFLUENCE

Listening is the most important skill a leader can master. When you listen for meaning and understanding rather than just the words, you can learn what motivates people; you can understand problems and their causes; you can discover opportunities for training; you can garner respect; and, you can gain insight into the best ways to get people to do what you want them to do.

Opportunities can best be discovered when you interact with others and really listen. To really listen, you need to stop talking, clear your mind of distractions or extraneous thoughts, and stay in the moment.

To recognize opportunities, you need to put your own assumptions on a back burner. People have very different points of view, and they will be able to see opportunities that you don't see. Resist the temptation to pre judge ideas presented by others because they do not have as much experience or education as you do. Conversely, set a goal to learn something from every encounter with another individual. When you keep an open mind and actively seek insight, you will automatically become a better listener.

Many conflicts or misunderstandings are caused because one or both parties in a conversation haven't listened. Perhaps one person thought they knew what the other person was thinking and jumped to a conclusion. Or, they were so focused on what they wanted to say that they missed the main point. When conflicts do arise, or tempers flare, don't immediately start defending yourself or start attacking. Instead, commit to giving the other person five minutes or whatever seems appropriate, to state his or her case. Really listen. Perhaps the person just needs to vent; or, there might be a legitimate issue or concern which needs to be addressed.

As the other person talks through their thoughts, two

things will happen: 1) They will feel better about the situation almost immediately; and 2) you gain some insight into how to resolve the problem.

THE POWER OF PERSUASION

Credibility is probably the most important ingredient in persuading someone. Does the other person like you, understand you, believe you, and trust you? Do you have a reputation for honesty and integrity? Do you say what you will do and do what you say?

When you want to persuade someone, be prepared. Have all the available facts and information you need before you approach the other person. Try to anticipate possible objections and reactions and be prepared to deal with them. Enter every situation with positive expectancy. People can read your mind and that's good, because you can determine what's in your mind for them to read.

Try to look at the situation from the other person's perspective. What do they want and why do they want it? When you help enough other people get what they want, you will get what you want.

People are more likely to be persuaded when they believe someone sincerely cares about them and their ideas. Consequently, it is important to be a motivational listener. When it comes to persuasion, listening is as powerful, if not more powerful, than talking.

In addition, help people feel safe. When people are threatened, they will either become defensive, argumentative, and hostile, or they will withdraw, either mentally or physically. Reassure the other person of your mutual interest and help him or her be right.

POSITIVE CONFRONTING

Even in the best motivational environments, there will be occasions when an individual's behavior is inappropriate. On those occasions, it is important to confront the individual so he or she will stop the inappropriate behavior.

Unfortunately, many people think confrontation is negative. Childhood sayings run through their mind – for example, "If you cannot say anything nice about someone, don't say anything at all," or "Play nice." These thoughts can get in the way of appropriate confrontation.

If someone's behavior is inappropriate, you do him or her a disservice by not bringing it to his or her attention. Most, if not all, people want to know if their behavior is counter-productive for achieving the desired results.

To effectively handle confrontation, focus on specific issues or behaviors an individual can control and avoid personal attacks. Be sure to avoid using rumors, innuendos, or sarcasm as a basis for confronting the individual by dealing with the facts.

When confronting someone, avoid inflammatory words such as should, ought to, have to, always, never, etc. Instead, focus on desired goals, results, and appropriate behavior. As you deliver information, train yourself to listen for what's important or key to the issue.

Be direct without being rude, obnoxious, or otherwise offensive. Treat the individual with dignity and respect and never show your anger. Remember, people will always remember how you made them feel long after the specific words are forgotten.

TAKING DISCIPLINARY ACTION

The main purpose of disciplinary action is to stop or correct inappropriate behavior. Inappropriate behavior could be described as any behavior that is counter-productive to the achievement of the team's or the organization's goals. It also would include any behavior that threatens the safety or well-being of other team members, customers, or the general public.

It is natural to view taking disciplinary action as negative or adversarial. However, if correcting the behavior is in the best interest of the team, the organization, and, ultimately, the team member, it can be viewed as positive and helpful.

If your organization already has a written procedure for administering discipline, we recommend that you use it. Feel free to use any of the following ideas to improve your procedure. If you do not have a written procedure, you will find the following guidelines useful.

Disciplinary action needs to be taken as soon after the cause as possible
Make sure your facts are accurate, and you can support your action.

The disciplinary action should never be a surprise to the person receiving the discipline
If it is clear what inappropriate behavior is and what the consequences of violations are, the individual can only blame themself for the consequences.

Disciplinary action needs to be consistent
Allow for extenuating circumstances. Is this a first time offense? Is the person remorseful? What is the likelihood that this behavior will be repeated?

Disciplinary action needs to be objective and impersonal
Remain calm and non-defensive. Address the behavior; do not attack the person.

Treat all employees with dignity and respect, regardless of your personal feelings toward them. Fairness is in the eyes of the beholder. When you play favorites, people will perceive that you are not fair.

GAINING COMMITMENT

Commitment is not something that can be observed directly. However, there are two things we can observe when it comes to commitment: 1) committed people appear to be focused in doing their work; and, 2) committed people are willing to make personal sacrifices to reach their team's goals.

Competence is an important ingredient for gaining commitment. People do not like to fail. They will avoid the things they think they cannot do. Therefore, it is important that you make certain that people have the ability and willingness to be successful. To do this, ensure that people have the knowledge, skills, experience, and confidence to perform their jobs.

Another important ingredient for gaining commitment is "ownership." People will perform better and be more committed when they have input on how to do their jobs and feel that they can influence outcomes.

Perhaps the most important ingredient in gaining the commitment of others is showing appreciation. When "appreciation" is included in employee satisfaction surveys, it is usually one of the lowest ranked items. Early in my career, I heard a lot of managers say, "The appreciation you get for doing a good job is that you get to keep your job." That strategy didn't work then, and it is even less effective today. People do their best work when they believe that what they do matters.

The good news is that showing appreciation for outstanding performance is relatively easy. Showing appreciation for improved performance is harder because you have to be observant enough, and have a good enough scorekeeping system in place, to notice the improvement.

Where most leaders struggle the most is showing appreciation for consistent, steady, continuing performance. The thing we hear the most about showing appreciation for people doing their jobs consistently is, "That's what they get paid to do. Why should we show them appreciation for doing what they are paid to do?"

The reason you want to show them appreciation, beyond their paycheck, is so they will continue to do what you pay them to do. As a bonus, you will gain greater commitment in the process. It's worth the time and effort.

Have you ever met someone who feels over-appreciated at work? Have you ever felt over-appreciated? Most people, in the workforce, feel under-appreciated. Anything you can do to help others feel appreciated will pay big dividends in improving performance, increasing productivity, creating a motivational environment, and getting greater results.

To give your appreciation a little more zing, make it personal. Instead of just sending an e-mail or letter, call the individual; instead of just calling the person, go see him or her. Think of creative ways to personalize the appreciation such as a one-of-a-kind certificate with a message unique to the accomplishment of that individual. If the person is a NASCAR fan, create a certificate in the name of his or her favorite driver or present something that signifies that driver's accomplishments.

HOW TO CELEBRATE SUCCESSES... INCLUDING IMPROVEMENT

There are several different types of success that should always be celebrated.

Outstanding performance is the most visible and

therefore the most recognized. When someone does something outstanding, it is usually obvious to everyone and is easy to recognize and give positive feedback.

Improved performance, on the other hand, usually isn't as obvious. Sometimes even individuals are not aware of areas where they have improved. An effective leader takes notice of improved performance and offers praise. It is worth the effort because praise improves performance and encourages more of the same.

The hardest performance to celebrate is consistent performance. Too many times a person who is a consistent performer is taken for granted. However, the best way to get continued consistent performance is to recognize the consistent performance. Most business people know that customers go where they are wanted and stay where they are appreciated. Individuals do the same thing. Taking good people for granted is a form of disrespect and does not bring out the best in people.

Consider the following when you are celebrating successes:

Personalize
When celebrating successes and improvements, be specific. Recognize the overall accomplishment and each team member's contribution.

Promptly
"Wait" is a four letter word that means nothing when it comes to celebrating successes and improvement. Even if there will be a formal celebration later, it is important to give informal recognition promptly after success occurs.

Re-live
Remembering past successes and replaying them can keep the motivation level high and help emphasize to your team members that you value their contributions.

Have employees tell how they did it

Getting employees to tell you and others how they accomplished something reinforces the success feeling they experienced at the time and shows that you value them and their performance.

Give symbolic prizes

Giving prizes that remind the achiever of the accomplishment will lengthen the celebration. For example, if an employee or the team cuts time out of a process that results in considerable financial savings and/or better customer service, a watch or clock with a commemorative message will be an ongoing reminder of the success.

AUTHORITY AND INFLUENCE - SUMMARY

✓ Titles are usually bestowed, but authority must be earned.

✓ Listening is the most important skill a manager or supervisor can master.

✓ A problem arises when those with power refuse to cooperate.

✓ Personal power is dependant on our own choice and determination to deliberately change our own behaviors.

✓ Perhaps the most important ingredient in gaining the commitment of team members is showing appreciation.

AUTHORITY AND INFLUENCE - AFFIRMATIONS

✓ I actively listen to others.

✓ I avoid using anger or "scolding" tactics.

✓ I energize others.

✓ I show appreciation for outstanding performance.

✓ I celebrate successes.

18.
Guarding Your Integrity

"Character is what you really are; reputation is only what others believe you to be."

Once there was an emperor in the Far East who was growing old and knew it was coming time to choose his successor. Instead of choosing one of his assistants or one of his own children, he decided to do something different.

He called all the young people in the kingdom together one day. He said, "It has come time for me to step down and to choose the next emperor. I have decided to choose one of you." The kids were shocked! But the emperor continued. "I am going to give each one of you a seed today. One seed. It is a very special seed. I want you to go home, plant the seed, water it, and come back here one year from today with what you have grown from this one seed. I will then judge the plants that you bring to me, and the one I choose will be the next emperor of the kingdom!"

There was one boy named Ling who was there that day and he, like the others, received a seed. He went home and excitedly told his mother the whole story. She helped him get a pot and some planting soil, and he planted the seed and watered it carefully. Every day, he would water it and watch to see if it had grown.

After about three weeks, some of the other youths began to talk about their seeds, and the plants that were beginning to grow. Ling kept going home and checking his seed, but nothing ever grew. Three weeks, four weeks, five weeks went by. Still nothing.

By now others were talking about their plants but Ling didn't have a plant, and he felt like a failure. Six months went by, still nothing in Ling's pot. He just knew he had killed his seed. Everyone else had trees and tall plants, but he had nothing. Ling didn't say anything to his friends; however, he just kept waiting for his seed to grow.

A year finally went by and all the youths of the kingdom brought their plants to the emperor for inspection. Ling told his mother that he wasn't going to take an empty pot. But she encouraged him to go, and to take his pot, and to be honest about what happened. Ling felt sick to his stomach, but he knew his mother was right. He took his empty pot to the palace.

When Ling arrived, he was amazed at the variety of plants grown by all the other youths. They were beautiful, in all shapes and sizes. Ling put his empty pot on the floor, and many of the other kinds laughed at him. A few felt sorry for him and just said, "Hey, nice try."

When the emperor arrived, he surveyed the room and greeted the young people. Ling just tried to hide in the back. "My, what great plants, trees, and flowers you have grown," said the emperor. "Today, one of you will be appointed the next emperor!"

All of a sudden, the emperor spotted Ling at the back of the room with his empty pot. He ordered his guards to bring him to the front. Ling was terrified. "The emperor knows I'm a failure! Maybe he will have me killed!"

When Ling got to the front, the Emperor asked his name. "My name is Ling," he replied. All the kids were laughing and making fun of him. The emperor asked everyone to quiet down. He looked at Ling and then announced to the crowd, "Behold your new emperor! His name is Ling!" Ling couldn't believe it. Ling couldn't even grow his seed. How could he be the new emperor?

Then the emperor said, "One year ago today, I gave everyone here a seed. I told you to take the seed, plant it, water it, and bring it back to me today. But I gave you all boiled seeds which would not grow. All of you, except Ling, have brought me trees and plants and flowers. When you found that the seed would not grow, you substituted another seed for the one I gave you. Ling was the only one with the courage and honesty to bring me a pot with my seed in it. Therefore, he is the one who will be the new emperor!"

LEADING WITH INTEGRITY

Integrity is the cornerstone of trust, and trust is the cornerstone of all relationships. Therefore, trust and integrity are essential in order to develop your personal leadership.

Integrity is doing the right thing because it is the right thing to do. It can also be defined as doing the right thing even if no one will ever find out or even if you don't get credit for doing it. Integrity is saying what you will do and doing what you said.

Integrity demands that when you make a mistake, you own it, admit it, fix it, and move on. People who don't understand the power of integrity spend more time and energy covering up or denying a mistake than they would admitting it, fixing it, and moving on.

HOLD YOURSELF ACCOUNTABLE DAILY

Unfortunately, most people think they hold themselves accountable, when in reality they are usually looking for someone or something else to blame.

When my son was 3 or 4, he was sitting on the floor in front of the TV eating a meal. His food and milk were on a tray over his legs. His older sister was sitting several feet away. When my son accidentally spilled his milk, he turned immediately to his sister and said, "See what you made me do!" His sister hadn't done or said a thing and wasn't close enough to touch the tray anyway. Even at a young age, people have a tendency to look for someone or something to blame other than themselves.

We've all heard that when we point one finger at someone else, there are three pointing back at us. We need to keep this in mind when things don't turn out the way we want. Instead of trying to affix blame, search for ways to fix the problem or repair the damage. Even if it wasn't your fault, you can be 100 percent accountable for figuring out how to make things better. Remember, it's not your situation; it's your reaction to the situation that really matters.

In difficult situations, ask yourself:

- "What can I do to make a difference?"
- "How can I add value?"
- "What can I do to help?"
- "What can I do differently to affect the outcome?"
- "What could I do different next time?"
- "What can I learn from this?"
- "What else can I do?"

COMMUNICATING WITH INTEGRITY

As we discussed previously, most people think they are better communicators than they really are. As a result, deadlines are missed, productivity suffers, mistakes are made, feelings get hurt, tempers flare, customers leave, and profits sag.

How would your life be better if you and everyone you interacted with improved their communication from good to great? With more messages than ever before flying at us from all directions, even being a good communicator isn't good enough these days. The gap between being a **good** communicator and being a **great** communicator can be huge.

Great communication is more than keeping people informed. Great communication requires that people respond to your ideas, direction, and leadership. They respond to how you look (including your demeanor and expression), how you act, what you say, and how you say it.

Fortunately, you have total control over how you look, how you act, what you say, and how you say it. That means you have total control over your side of any communication. Since people respond to these four factors, and you can control them, the better you communicate, the higher the chance of getting people to respond to your ideas, direction, and leadership.

Listed below are seven ways you can improve your communication ability and lead with integrity:

Choose your words and phrasing carefully (what you say).

Words are powerful. They can build up or tear down, encourage or discourage, clarify or confuse, motivate or demotivate. Choose simple, easy to understand words that clarify, build up, encourage and motivate. Instead of "should have" (judgmental), say "next time." Instead of "have to" (parental), say, "get to" or "it's important." Instead of "always" or "never," use specific occurrences. Phrases such as, "I believe in you," "I appreciate you," "tell me about it," and "thank you" are powerful and get people to respond to you in a positive manner.

232 DEVELOPING PERSONAL LEADERSHIP

Choose tone and inflection carefully (how you say it).
"WHAT.... WERE... YOU... THINKING?" will illicit a different response than "What happened?" or "Tell me about it." Tone and inflection can help emphasize key points. Improper use can also trigger negative emotions. Remember, people will remember how you made them feel (positive or negative) long after they forget the words you used.

Choose facial expressions and body language that are congruent with your message (how you look and how you act).
People will put credence in what they see over what they hear. Make eye contact. Stay in the moment (avoid looking at your watch, checking your voice or text messages, or otherwise disrespecting the other person). Avoid posture or gestures that might indicate you'd rather be somewhere else.

Choose to listen purposely and actively with your eyes as well as your ears.
Eliminate or reduce distractions, take notes, ask questions, paraphrase for understanding, and do anything else to ensure you fully understand what the other person is saying, needs, and means. Listen to word choice, phrasing, and what the person is not saying in addition to what he or she is saying. Your eyes can help by reading facial expressions and body language. My granddaughter (who is five) can read facial expressions and body language – and she's never attended a body language course. If she can do it, you can too.

Choose to communicate with integrity.
The truth will find you out. If you haven't been truthful, your credibility will be damaged. Besides, it is easier to tell the truth because you don't have to remember what you said. When you communicate with integrity, you will feel better about yourself and be more effective in every area of your business and life.

Choose to be a positive, enthusiastic communicator.
Positive, enthusiastic people attract people, and negative, dull people have a tendency to repel people. Choose to be the former.

Choose to ask better questions to get better answers.
When you have a reason for the communication, you have the tendency to ask better questions and get better answers. Plan your questions in advance and/or have an arsenal of questions that have proven effective in given situations.

Take a minute to notice that each of these actions is a choice. Choosing to communicate with integrity will help you become a better leader.

EMPATHY/EGO BALANCE

As a leader, it is important that you maintain a balance between empathy and ego.

Empathy is the ability to know how other people are feeling. Ego is the desire to win. A formula for effective communication could be stated as:

EMPATHY + EGO = EFFECTIVE COMMUNICATION

Effective communication requires a proper balance of both empathy and ego.

When people have a great deal of empathy and very little ego, they might be great listeners, but they lack the drive to motivate other people to action.

On the other hand, when people have very little empathy and a lot of ego, they usually are poor listeners and are perceived as "bulldozers" – they want to win at any cost.

A proper balance allows people to be good listeners, understand other people's situations, ask the right questions, and suggest a winning course of action. A proper balance will improve your leadership ability.

234 DEVELOPING PERSONAL LEADERSHIP

DEALING WITH NEGATIVE PEOPLE AND RESISTANCE

All leaders, regardless of their ability, will encounter people who display negativity and resistance.

A person with a mental block has immediate resistance to your ideas without fully understanding what you have said. To overcome a mental block, you need to keep your goal firmly in mind – for example, to get the individual to do what you want. Do not argue with a mental block; it will only generate more defensiveness and reduce the chance of them seeing your point of view. Using logic on a closed mind is a waste of time.

To remove mental blocks, ask a specific question which causes the mental block to identify what is impeding communication. Some questions to ask could include:

» "What prevents us from…?"

» "If you were in my position, how would you respond?"

» "What evidence do you have that…?"

» "What conditions would have to exist to…?"

In addition, listen for block phrases, such as:

» "I can't"

» "It's impossible"

» "Have to"

» "As you know"

» "Should"

» "Ought to"

» "I'm so busy"

» "Obviously"

Pay attention to over generalizations, such as "never," "always," "everyone," "no one," and "all." When someone uses a generalization, ask, "Never? Has there ever been a time when …?" This will jog the mental block's mind to look for an exception that will diminish the strength of their argument. It is important that you don't get hooked on over-generalizations since this will give the individual's statements more validity than they deserve.

DEALING WITH CRITICISM

One of your most vulnerable moments is when someone criticizes you, and in a leadership role, it is guaranteed to happen. It is never comfortable to hear negative comments about yourself. Your natural tendency is to get emotional and fight (verbally) or flee either mentally or physically.

When dealing with criticism, do not leap to your own defense or counter-attack. Instead pause, allowing time for both of you to cool down and say, "I understand." Then, repeat the criticism, word for word, and ask for more information. For example, you can say, "What, specifically, leads you to that conclusion?" Or, thank the person for his feedback and ask him to tell you more. In the beginning, listen more and talk and move less. Keep your motions, voice, and tone lower and slower.

If you believe the comments are accurate, acknowledge it. If an apology is in order, sooner is better than later. Thank the individual for their feedback and tell them what you will do differently in the future. If you disagree with the comments, say, "May I present my perspective?" Then, do so.

If the above ideas do not satisfy the situation, try to move them to a problem-solving mode by asking, "What will make it better?" or "What would make it better for both of us?"

GUARDING YOUR INTEGRITY - SUMMARY

✓ Integrity is doing the right thing at the right time because it's the right thing to do.

✓ Communicating effectively and with integrity builds trust, and good relationships are built on trust.

✓ Listening effectively involves your eyes, mind, and intuition, as well as your ears.

✓ Holding yourself accountable for your thoughts and actions on a daily basis will deepen your integrity.

✓ Integrity is more of an attitude than a skill.

GUARDING YOUR INTEGRITY - AFFIRMATIONS

✓ I am a person of integrity.

✓ I am an effective communicator.

✓ I am a good listener. I listen to understand, learn, and pay respect.

✓ I am accountable for my thoughts and actions.

✓ I say what I will do and do what I say.